Wordsworth and the adequacy of landscape

'Wordsworth on Helvellyn' by
Benjamin Robert Haydon (1842)
National Portrait Gallery

Wordsworth and the adequacy of landscape

Donald Wesling

New York

Barnes & Noble, Inc.

First published in Great Britain 1970
Published in the United States of America 1970
by Barnes & Noble Inc., New York, N.Y.

ISBN 0 389 03995 0

Printed in Great Britain

To my Parents

Scenery is fine — but Human Nature is finer

       — John Keats, *Letters*

. . . he that suffers most desires
The red bird most and the strongest sky —

       — Wallace Stevens, 'On the Adequacy of
       Landscape'

Contents

Preface

This is an essay on description and meditation in landscape poetry. It describes the integration of two kinds of thinking, and a variety of beauties and lapses that come from their separation. An adequate literary representation of human life will, I suggest, inform description with meditation, and will be at once fully aesthetic and fully ethical. This notion of human and literary achievement is nothing new; the interest lies in watching Wordsworth as he employs — sternly, and, after 1798, more or less deliberately — just such a criterion to extend his range of concern from love of nature to love of mankind.

The essay is not, then, about Wordsworth's concept of nature; nor is it about his appropriation of the theory and practice of landscape gardening, or of theories of the Picturesque and the Sublime. Readers interested in Nature should consult J. W. Beach's account of Wordsworth in The Concept of Nature (1936), and Geoffrey Hartman's distinguished Wordsworth's Poetry 1787–1814 (1964); those interested in technical questions of landscape painting and gardening should consult Russell Noyes's Wordsworth and the Art of Landscape (1968).

My essay owes much to studies of Wordsworth by John Jones, Donald Davie, David Ferry, David Perkins, C. C. Clarke, and Geoffrey Hartman; and to the advice of Gabriel Pearson, George Dekker, Anthony Heilbut, and especially David Perkins. Acknowledgement is due to Texas Studies in Literature and Language (University of Texas) and to English Literary History (Johns Hopkins), for permission to reprint portions of articles already published. The text quoted throughout and abbreviated *PW* is *The Poetical Works of William Wordsworth*, edited by Ernest de Selincourt and Helen Darbishire, five volumes (Oxford, 1949–58). The text of *The Prelude* used is that edited by Ernest de Selincourt and revised by Helen Darbishire (Oxford, 1959); the 1850 version is used throughout, except where 1805 is explicitly noted. .

D.W

I

The early poems: achieving habits of meditation

I

The path to the great Romantic writers is still not clear. The impasse, of course, is the impression left by two decades of writing between the wars – brilliant, eccentric in tendency, programmatic – when the focal object of writing was direct treatment of the thing. This meant a decision to condense poems into images: and often it meant the banishing of concepts in fear of the Romantic excesses of over-statement or vagueness. 'Always seek the hard, definite, personal word,' said T. E. Hulme; 'Go in fear of abstractions,' said Ezra Pound: 'The proper and perfect symbol is the natural object.' The revolutionary experiments of Pound and Eliot, reinforced by a cor-responding preference in the universities for Donne, the Symbolists, and Hopkins, remain unchallenged even today as 'modern poetry' in English. And this despite the disagreement of more recent poets who, believing the revolution is over and needs to be studied in the lessons of its triumphs and mistakes, yet do not want 'simply to take up', as Thom Gunn has said, 'where Hardy left off' (*Yale Review*, Spring, 1964).

Now if as Gunn says 'poetry is impoverished unless one can in-clude the whole of one's attempt to understand the world, concepts as well as images', certainly Wordsworth as the greatest connector of the previous century, interested as he was in demonstrating the con-nective and persuasive powers of the mind, will be an instructive writer for anyone who believes great poetry must coadunate image and discourse, matter and principle, thing and idea. His arrangement of continuity in meditative structures as compressed as 'Tintern Abbey' and as extensive as *The Prelude*, the expertness of his transitions – 'no superficial or merely technical matter', says Gunn, 'for the transitions are between thought and imagery' – make him a larger, more capacious version of ourselves when he is at his best, a poet who without any fastidious embroidery gets down to the profoundly moral job of understanding the encounters of mind and world.

I shall try to show in the following pages the moral and technical implications of Wordsworth's conscious attempt to perfect a landscape genre which had been developing in the half-century before his birth. My inquiry concerns the adequacy of landscape as the mediator of a full image of man; and the adequacy of landscape as a literary vehicle which modifies the technical resources of a meditative poet.

Any use of the term 'adequacy' will imply a criterion of excellence, as for example when Matthew Arnold writing 'On the Modern Element in Literature' asks, 'Has [Virgil's *Aeneid*] the depth, the completeness of the poems of Aeschylus or Sophocles, of those adequate and consummate representations of human life?' To substitute *The Prelude* for the *Aeneid* and Shakespeare for 'Aeschylus or Sophocles' will begin to clarify my own use of 'adequacy'. I take over Arnold's strenuous and humane definition as my own. For Arnold, the union of 'a significant, a highly developed, a culminating epoch' with a comprehensive literature makes for adequacy of interpretation:

> Now, the peculiar characteristic of the highest literature –
> the poetry – of the fifth century in Greece before the Christian era, is its *adequacy*; the peculiar characteristic of the poetry of Sophocles is its consummate, its unrivalled _adequacy_; that it represents the highly developed human nature of that age – human nature developed in a number of directions, politically, socially, religiously, morally developed – in its completest and most harmonious development in all these directions; while there is shed over this poetry the charm of that noble serenity which always accompanies true insight.

If we inspect Wordsworthian landscape with Arnold's criterion of 'human nature developed in a number of directions', we quickly find it inadequate by comparison with Sophocles or Shakespeare. The description of dead matter, perhaps given a slight animation by the projection of human sympathies, simply does not minister to a satisfying representation of human life. It is necessary, then, to pose the question somewhat differently: to ask how Wordsworth's growing determination to pronounce 'On man, on nature, and on human life' (praised by Arnold in his essay on Wordsworth) served by degrees to transform his earlier poetry of landscape. For the evidence of the poems is that Wordsworth himself perceived his earlier writing to be, in the sense of the term here described, inadequate.

Though occasionally, for clarity of exposition, I distinguish the human and poetic meanings of adequacy, of course the two meanings are united in Wordsworth's finest landscape writing. In his successful poems the moral and the technical preoccupation are defined one by the other. One instance which can stand for many comprises the opening lines of *The Prelude* where the poet, paraphrasing the last lines of *Paradise Lost* with something like a conscious self-critique, says 'The earth is all before me'. Then he spends almost the whole of the first of thirteen books trying to find a subject, describing in fact the impasse of the man who, aspiring to write an epic, has only himself and the visible world as his materials. He admits to being exposed, directionless:

> . . . whither shall I turn
> By road or pathway or through open field,
> Or shall a twig or any floating thing
> Upon the river, point me out my course?
>
> (version of 1805, I, ll. 29–32)

A poetry which must gesture 'here' and 'there' at the external world will inevitably encounter such difficult questions of ordonnance. The most serious disadvantage of landscape as a literary vehicle emerges from the implied elevation of the prospect over a literal spread of appearance and a whole field of memory. The earth is all before the poet, yet he must ask 'whither shall I turn?'

Since the question – of how to get from image to discourse, or more broadly of how to express a significant apprehension of the world – is pre-eminently one of method, we are fortunate to have two remarkable statements to rely on. Here is Dr. Johnson, commenting on the structure of Thomson's *Seasons*:

> The great defect of *The Seasons* is want of method; but for this I know not that there was any remedy. Of many appearances subsisting all at once, no rule can be given why one should be mentioned before another; yet the memory wants the help of order, and the curiosity is not excited by suspense or expectation.
>
> ('Life of Thomson')

This is very likely unanswerable as an analysis of why it is that whole

3

poems will not come of the attempt to build up a world by versified catalogue. Nevertheless, for Johnson a poem is still to be regarded as a reflection or imitation of an autonomous order outside itself; he cannot conceive any remedy for 'want of method'.

We are taken further by Coleridge's brilliant treatise 'On Method'. Here Coleridge asks how we distinguish, even among educated men, 'the man of superior mind'; and he answers:

> It is the unpremeditated and evidently habitual arrange-
> ment of his words, grounded on the habit of foreseeing,
> in each integral part, or (more plainly) in every sentence,
> the whole that he then intends to communicate. However
> irregular and desultory his talk, there is method in the
> fragments.

If 'absence of method' is occasioned by 'an habitual submission of the understanding to mere events and images as such', method on the other hand 'becomes natural to the mind which has been accustomed to contemplate not things only, or for their own sake, but likewise and chiefly the relations of things, either their relations to each other, or to the observer, or to the state and apprehension of the hearers'. Method thus consists of a striving after genuine relationships. The excellence of Shakespeare's art, for instance, consists in a 'just proportion', a 'union and interpenetration . . . of the universal and the particular'.

So much might be expected from any Romantic theorist, but what follows on this could only have come from a man habitually obsessed by what he called 'the streamy nature of association':

> For method implies a progressive transition, and it is the
> meaning of the word in the original language. The Greek
> μέθοδος is literally a way or path of transit. . . . As
> without continuous transition there can be no method, so
> without a preconception there can be no transition with
> continuity. The term, method, cannot therefore, otherwise
> than by abuse, be applied to a mere dead arrangement,
> containing in itself no principle of progression.

There is a closely related sentence in the essay 'On Poesy or Art':

> Remember that there is a difference between form as pro-
> ceeding, and shape as superinduced; – the latter is either
> the death or the imprisonment of the thing; – the former
> is its self-witnessing and self-effected sphere of agency.

4

Method as 'progressive transition' and form 'as proceeding' are the operative definitions, but it is also essential to take the force of concepts such as 'relation' and 'preconception' – so as to be very clear that the process Coleridge describes is not uncontrolled but the graph of a particular sort of intellection. Before the writing of 'Tintern Abbey' in mid-1798, Wordsworth is in search of just such a measured, methodical discourse. He achieves it, in that poem, by taking for meditation a scene full of intense personal meaning, and by dwelling on certain unique but representative moments when the feel of the facts has been extraordinary. Moreover, the poem's vocabulary, syntax, and prosody, blending image and discourse, make the technical solution inseparable from the moral one.

Now poets in any given period will usually differ greatly in the degree to which they crave the authority of received poetic forms. Yet it does seem generally true that poetry has moved from a highly determinate period style in the age of Pope (heroic couplet, enclosed quatrain, epigram and maximal closure) to a hazardous but salutary freedom in the modern age (blank verse, free verse, the concrete poem and minimal closure). Again, in an acute period of crisis and redefinition for ordinary language and ordinary logic, such as the late eighteenth and early twentieth centuries, the related question of poetic structure will also be profoundly vexed. In *The Subtler Language* (1959) Earl Wasserman has remarked how especially revealing it is that the one 'organizing scheme the later eighteenth century developed, and the one from which it drew its greatest sense of meaningful order, was associationism'. The many versified catalogues of the time were extended indefinitely by a controlling concept wherein all objects, persons, and events were possibly significant to all others; writers of descriptive poems were unable to integrate the syntax of their description with the syntax of their moralizing, unable, as Wasserman says, to 'generate a new syntax' in the broadest sense, 'without which there is no poem, and no need for one'. This is a situation very similar to the one enunciated by those desperate fragments called 'Cinders' and placed towards the end of Hulme's *Speculations*; and 'clear-cut images', in Richard Aldington's phrase, or the image defined by Pound as 'an emotional and intellectual complex in an instant of time', seem calculated deliberately to evade the connective powers of the mind.

The disability shared by Hulme, H. D., Aldington, Flint, Fletcher, Amy Lowell, even Ezra Pound at times, with Thomson and Cowper and the versifying topographers, is this: however superb they may be at producing images, they have not the procedures to co-ordinate them. Though Imagism is a subtler, post-Romantic form of Associationism, though Imagist poems are not as a rule barnacled-over with a poetic diction, the Imagist poem shares with the later-Augustan poem the lack of a principle of progression. *The Seasons* is flawed from first to last by its inept transitions, while *The Complete Poetical Works of T. E. Hulme* set out systematically to suppress all transitions. Thomson, like Hulme, has no controlling concept, no syntax in the widest sense which will render perceptions fully significant.

Romantic and post-Imagist poets, beginning to write in the midst of this dilemma, required a causality which would prefigure in all its transitions the effect which was the poem. The need to convert a series of perceptions into a continuous poem, and to interrelate part and whole, description and discourse, obliged them entirely to re-think the question of poetic structure. Moreover, this had to be accomplished in the process of writing poems, a task clearly more formidable for English Romantic writers, involving nothing less than a total crisis of personality in the poet as in his readership. 'I feel like the first men who read Wordsworth,' Randall Jarrell has said in a poem: 'It's so simple I can't understand it.' By observing more precisely how the description is absorbed within a larger context of purposeful meditation in the best of Wordsworth's poetry, and how this process determines progressive transition within the continuous poem, the modern reader can, I think, repossess something at least of this difficult simplicity.

2

In jocular seriousness Wordsworth wrote:

> Not in Utopia, – subterranean fields, –
> Or some secreted island, Heaven knows where!
> But in the very world, which is the world
> Of all of us, – the place where, in the end,
> We find our happiness, or not at all!
>
> (Prelude, XI, 11. 140–4)

Nothing that at all matters in the conditions of our perception and intellection has changed since Wordsworth wrote this, and the large

6

body of his major poetry which exists as evidence remains compelling and original. As in any writing which deals with landscape in its broadest definition, his poetry is at best a celebration of secular experience. Towards the end of the nineteenth century another landscape writer reminds himself to 'consider the Wordsworthian dictum (the more perfectly the natural object is reproduced, the more truly poetic the picture)'; but Thomas Hardy goes on not as Hulme or Pound would but in profoundly Romantic terms:

> This reproduction is achieved by seeing into the *heart of a thing* (as rain, wind, for instance), and is realism, in fact, though through being pursued by means of the imagination it is confounded with invention, which is pursued by the same means. It is, in short, reached by what M. Arnold calls 'the imaginative reason'.
>
> (Quoted in Florence Emily Hardy, *The Life of Thomas Hardy*, 1962)

From Wordsworth and the Wordsworthians Hardy learned to call poetic imagination reason in her most exalted mood. For both writers (as for Arnold too at mid-century) the creative process in poems and novels, a delicate balance between perception and imagination, lacked the mediation of an overarching metaphysic. This is in fact why they have resort to landscape, why they are always in the process of the Blakean cleansing of the doors of perception; the barely credible transcendence, the access of knowledge, comes from nowhere if it does not come from a specific place in the real world. And yet, it is true too and an index of Hardy's diminished sympathies and dun visions, that 'Minds that have nothing to confer/Find little to perceive' (*PW*, II, 25).

Often in the scope of a single essay, Victorian readers of Wordsworth like the later De Quincey, John Stuart Mill, J. C. Shairp, Stopford Brooke, Aubrey de Vere, Leslie Stephen, or F. T. Palgrave, expressed admiration for both the sensory acuity and the reflective power of Wordsworth. In certain passages where the poet is being most attentive to the natural world, says Aubrey de Vere, 'meditation and observation constitute a single intellectual act': no two faculties could be 'less like each other than those of meditation and observation' yet 'to Wordsworth they belonged alike'. De Quincey, one of the earliest intelligent commentators, says as much when he claims that 'scarcely has there been a poet with what could be called a learned eye, or an eye *extensively* learned before Wordsworth. . . . But

B

the great distinction of Wordsworth . . . is the extent of his sympathy for what is *really* permanent in human feelings, and also the depth of this sympathy'. Such testimonies, adduced because they show strong response to the descriptive and topographical elements of Wordsworth as well as to the massive moral elements, praise the integration of image and concept. They hint at the contention, not novel in criticism but rarely approached by way of a consistent focus on landscape, that the epistemological interest and very habit of charged vision leads inevitably, all but simultaneously, in this poet to ethical and religious concern. The seeing is itself evaluative, or becomes so; description is not permitted to exist for long without the abstracting and meditative modes of thought coming to inspect, enlarge, and dignify. Yet at best the descriptive is the base: 'The accuracy of accurate letters' is for Wordsworth as for Wallace Stevens 'an accuracy with respect to the structure of reality'.

Especially after meeting Coleridge, Wordsworth was alert to the equivocations of a poetry which discusses the transactions between mind and world. 'Thought and reality,' said Coleridge, 'are, as it were, two distinct corresponding sounds, of which no man can say positively which is the voice and which the echo'. Elsewhere Coleridge describes the meditative power as a focusing lens for the eye, a determinant of description: 'By *meditation*, rather than by *description*? And by the latter in consequence of the former? As eyes, for which the former has predetermined their field of vision, and to which, as to its origin, it communicates a microscopic power.' It is this 'armed vision' which explodes the Locke tradition and Hartleian mechanical associationism, 'for what is harmony but a mode of relation, the very *esse* of which is *percipi*? – an *ens rationale*, which presupposes the power, that by perceiving creates it'. As early as 1800 Wordsworth was defending himself by making it clear that his intentions in the *Lyrical Ballads* were not merely descriptive but moral, stating that if his theory of purposive description is wrong he 'can have little right to the name of a Poet': 'Not that I always begin to write with a distinct purpose formally conceived; but habits of meditation have, I trust, so prompted and regulated those feelings, that they will be found to carry along with them a *purpose*' (1800 Preface). There is, then, as a practical rationale for writing, a recognition generally of the primacy of the meditative intelligence – 'our thoughts, which are indeed the representatives of all our past feelings' – but of the intransigent necessity as well of those 'continued influxes of feeling' arising from our commerce with the world and its things and persons.

It is possible to illustrate Wordsworth's convictions by taking up other than moral topics – by discussing his use of landscape rather than his concept of nature – because to Wordsworth poems about ways of knowing objects and landscapes are also poems about how to live. There is scarcely one of his poems, he says, 'which does not aim to direct the attention to some moral sentiment, or to some general principle, or law of thought, or of our intellectual constitution'. The effectiveness, and the arbitrary fragility, of Wordsworthian 'habits of meditation' are illustrated in the same letter of 1807 in which this axiom is stated, where he shows how his sonnet 'With ships the sea was sprinkled far and nigh' is an example of the mind's tendency to fasten on a single object or pattern from among unmeaning multitude as an arbitrary principle of order. In the poem it is 'a lordly Ship' which obtrudes on his notice, making the others subordinate, though the poet, while enjoying his own spontaneous metaphor of king and subjects applied to ships, realizes fully that the ship 'was nought to me, nor I to her'. By a lucky glance, meaning and value have been won.

In most of the *Lyrical Ballads* the Romantic problem, to paraphrase Whitehead, of energizing with value the essence of matter of fact, was surmounted by the early Wordsworthian dramatic voice and by a preference for rural simplicity or human extremity. Wordsworth believed that under such conditions vision would come as a matter of course: one remembers in 'Anecdote for Fathers' the five-year-old who, pressed to give reasons for loving, teaches his father not to exploit human perception; the gentle 'Idiot Boy' whose glee it was to hear owls as crowing cocks and to feel a night-time sun shining cold; the 'Forsaken Indian Woman' who, ill and alone, hears the rustling and crackling of the northern lights. In *The Prelude* and other meditative pieces, those fully characteristic poems where the concern is not anecdotal but directly personal, the human value of a scene is conveyed in two ways. There is the deliberate scrutiny of a thing or place from an authentic vantage point until it reveals its mystery: as in the poem on a sighted ship assembling the sea or the beginnings of 'Lines left upon a Seat' and 'Tintern Abbey'. Or, there is the recreation of instantaneous insight in the past; often this comes after a period of dull physical exertion and relative impercipience: as in the fragment 'A Night Piece' or the vision following the Snowdon climb in *The Prelude*. Whether imagination is roused by chance encounter or by

9

deliberately framed perception of the part which may be taken for the whole, far more 'composition of appearance' is necessary in the meditative poem than in the dramatic poem on the psychology of moral sentiment. Unlike the *Lyrical Ballads*, these more personal poems, because in their larger structure they are invariably retrospective, have the advantage of dealing in lapsed time; and memory appears to be the medium which best naturalizes the objects of perception in meditative verse.

In 1804, when there was still undiminished hope for the production of a long meditative poem on man, nature, and human life, Coleridge wrote prophesying 'immortality to Wordsworth's projected *Recluse* as the first & finest philosophical Poem, if only it be (as it undoubtedly will be) a Faithful Transcript of his most august & innocent Life, of his own habitual Feelings & Modes of seeing and hearing'. Without at all discussing in this context the medium of poetry, its dependence on a received language and tradition, Coleridge, interested in the psychology of the creator, postulates a philosophical habit of feeling and seeing. In effect, he is saying that Wordsworth, keen as he is to the nuances of ordinary perception, sees always in the events and texture of his life a more general validity and boldly takes his personal experience as representative.

The importance, we may imagine, lies not in the particular subject-matter of that experience, for the generic term 'meditation' in Coleridge's own use designates rather a process of the mind. Coleridge and Wordsworth talk about 'Modes of seeing and hearing' and 'habits of meditation' with the intention of keeping an anchor in the world of common perception while at the same time guarding themselves from the possible despotism of the outer senses. Wordsworth's best poetry preserves this equilibrium: in the habit of tranced attention watching a poised butterfly or a child's grave for half an hour, or repeating again and again 'I gazed – and gazed' ('I wandered Lonely as a cloud'); in the notion, often expressed, that there is a faculty of creation in the organs of outer sense (e.g., 'All the mighty world/Of eye, and ear, – both what they half create,/And what perceive'); in the ambivalence of 'vision' and the interlocking languages of 'thing' and 'thought', a sheer catalogue often alive in the midst of philosophical rhetoric. 'For sensation itself is but vision nascent,' said Coleridge, 'not the cause of intelligence but intelligence itself revealed as an earlier power in the process of self-construction' (*Biographia Literaria*, Chapter XII).

3

As early as 1794, while in his last term of residence at Cambridge, Coleridge saw 'the emergence of an original poetic genius' in the style and imagery of Wordsworth's recently published 'Descriptive Sketches' (1793). About this poem he remarks in the *Biographia Literaria*: 'In the form, style, and manner of the whole . . . and in the structure of the particular lines and periods, there is a harshness and acerbity connected and combined with words and images all aglow', such that the poem may be compared to the 'hard and thorny rind and shell, within which the rich fruit is elaborating'. What Coleridge implies as he continues is that descriptive poetry in this piece was being crammed with new perceptions and a fund of interest for the first time, a lesser genre bearing the energy and attention of a major one: 'The language is not only peculiar and strong, but at times knotty and contorted, as by its own impatient strength; while the novelty and struggling crowd of images, acting in conjunction with the difficulties of the style, demands always a greater closeness of attention, than poetry – at all events than descriptive poetry – has a right to claim.' That 'novelty and struggling crowd of images', implying an extremely high specific density of noticing, is most certainly in this poem a nascent vision, if not yet a fully armed one.

Wordsworth at the outset of the poem discusses human happiness in terms of the features of a God-given landscape, the first of many 'spots of holy ground' in his poetry, a place

> Where falls the purple morning far and wide
> In flakes of light upon the mountain-side;
> Where summer Suns in ocean sink to rest,
> Or moonlight Upland lifts her hoary breast;
> Where Silence, on her wing of night o'erbroods
> Unfathom'd dells and undiscover'd woods;
> Where rocks and groves the power of waters shakes
> In cataracts, or sleeps in quiet lakes.
>
> (version of 1793, 11. 5–12)

Every couplet has a new and different act of attention, and an authentic though stylized reference to the scene: concrete images in catalogue, representative here of the whole poem, carry the meaning along, with the slight directional pressure of the listed 'Where' changing the scene at the beginning of every couplet. The lines move from an almost impressionist observation in 'flakes of light', through twilight and silencing moonlight with such words as 'unfathom'd' and 'undiscover'd' designed to reveal the bosky strangeness of things, and finally there is only the night-time sound of moving waters.

In revising this poem in 1794 and much later (some time between 1832–1836), Wordsworth never tampered with the imagery, except to make its expression clearer and more precise where possible. By then, I think, he knew there was nothing wrong with the noticing in the poem; it was true so far as it went; what was wrong, rather, was the ordonnance. This was of course partly due to his choice of the traditional loco-descriptive heroic couplet, but also to a persistent attempt to crowd his lines with visual data. Still writing in the general mode of the Picturesque, he has not yet learned how to defeat the 'despotic' bodily eye. So the style itself tends to catalogue and writhe, to embellish rather than simplify the forms of things. Scenes of mild and fearful beauty, light and chiaroscuro, tend almost systematically to alternate, disjunction being signalled by unsubtle changes of pace: 'From such romantic dreams my soul awake,/Lo! Fear looks silent down on Uri's lake' (11. 283–4). At the Gondo Gorge we are invited to

> Plunge with the Russ embrown'd by Terror's breath,
> Where danger roofs the narrow walks of death;
> By floods, that, thundering from their dizzy height,
> Swell more gigantic on the stedfast sight;
> Black drizzling craggs, that beaten by the din,
> Vibrate, as if a voice complain'd within;
> Bare steeps, where Desolation stalks, afraid,
> Unstedfast, by a blasted yew upstay'd. . . .
>
> (version of 1793, 11. 245–52)

When Wordsworth rewrote this in 1799 as the blank verse fragment 'The Simplon Pass', later fitted into *The Prelude* as the culmination of sublime landscape feeling, he preserved the speaking crags but cut almost everything else, treating the danger of the scene rather by implication and adding a magnificent generalizing close. But in 1793 he had not yet taught himself the uses of the blank verse line for continuity, or the new language of blending or interfusion of the major poems after 1798. The flickering scenes of the journey poem, digressions on social questions, contorted syntax and an unexpected turn to dramatic situation at the end preclude any settled and ruminative intellection. In hesitating whether to attempt a painterly job on alpine scenes, flashing varied landscapes and digressive material before the reader, or to describe from his own point of view and limited perspective a journey he had himself taken, he writes a poem which owes allegiance to each ideal yet makes no plausible transitions between them.

The poem, displaying a *tour de force* of observation but only rudimentary habits of meditation, is a crucial one in the development of a theory of description. Manifestly, the lesson learned from its writing was that 'progressive transition' could not be prosecuted with the snapshot stasis of the Popian couplet and the painterly assumptions of theorists of the Picturesque like William Gilpin or Uvedale Price. Coleridge in an early diary note said of the Picturesque writer Erasmus Darwin that his poetry, because it relies too much on the sister art, 'makes the great little':

> Dr. Darwin's poetry, ~~makes~~ [sic] a succession of Landscapes or Paintings – it arrests the attention too often and so prevents the rapidity necessary to pathos. . . .
> – seems to have written his poems as Painters who of beautiful objects – take – studies.
>
> (*Notebooks*, ed. K. Coburn, 1957, entry 132)

Sheer aggregation is always the possible vice of a literature with the descriptive as its premise.

This is why Coleridge and Wordsworth defend transition, connection, coadunation, imaginative grasp of the unity of the impression; and why Wordsworth, in footnoting the stormy sunset passage in this poem, says he cannot apply the 'cold rules of painting' to the scene. He 'had once given to these sketches the title of Picturesque; but the Alps are insulted in applying to them that term' because the sublime images they evoke must always 'disdain the pencil'. Wordsworth sets the sublime against the picturesque, Burke against Gilpin, when he denies that painting can capture the scene, and instead consults 'nature and my feelings' by excluding from his description all hints of shade (to Gilpin, chiaroscuro technique was part of picturesque irregularity); in this way Wordsworth preserves the unity and grandeur of the impression, 'that deluge of light, or rather of fire, in which nature had wrapped the immense forms around me'.

The sunset storm is introduced abruptly:

> 'Tis storm; and hid in mist from hour to hour
> All day the floods a deeper murmur pour,
> And mournful sounds, as of a Spirit lost,
> Pipe wild along the hollow-blustering coast,
> 'Till the Sun walking on his western field
> Shakes from behind the clouds his flashing shield.
> Triumphant on the bosom of the storm,
> Glances the fire-clad eagle's wheeling form;
> Eastward, in long perspective glittering, shine
> The wood-crown'd cliffs that o'er the lake recline;
> Wide o'er the Alps a hundred streams unfold,
> At once to pillars turn'd that flame with gold;
> Behind his sail the peasant strives to shun
> The west that burns like one dilated sun,
> Where in a mighty crucible expire
> The mountains glowing hot, like coals of fire.
>
> (version of 1793, ll. 332–47)

Aided by the most flexible couplets of the poem, the sequence of images is a true progress ordered by the 'long perspective' of an elevated prospect. A single organizing consciousness is more strongly implied than elsewhere in the poem, as the movement proceeds from wide to narrow focus to include a human figure, from east to opposing west, from streams hidden but heard to streams actually seen unfolding. There is more than ordinary alpine topography in his images of clearing mists, the fiery eagle, the 'crucible' of the mountains, an interaction of earth and heavens which is the keynote of Wordsworth's greatest landscape writing.

Coleridge saw the presence of Wordsworthian bestowal so great here as to hazard that the scene may be 'an emblem of the poem itself, and of the author's genius as it was then displayed'. Though Coleridge may rely overmuch on retrospective reasoning when he fancies this, it is possible at least to affirm in this instance a prelusive blending of descriptive and meditative modes. The poem as a whole takes a step beyond the picturesque formulae, though the 'impatient strength' of the syntax, the presence of decorative gypsies and banditti, even the disconnection of individual sketches have close affinity with the tradition of the Picturesque. Clearly, Wordsworth is more interested in the landscape than in people; in this poem and in the earlier 'Evening Walk' he manages to include social commentary – in the manner of

Thomson and Cowper – only in digressions from description. Only after the period 1795–8 can he make larger personal and social concerns grow out of the presented scene, weighting descriptive poetry with the evoked significances of 'things'. Yet to effect this a radical change of language and procedure was necessary.

While he was revising 'An Evening Walk' and 'Descriptive Sketches' in 1794 at Windy Brow, coming slowly by way of revision to an appreciation of the representative use of landscape imagery, he was at the same time working up a narrative in Spenserian stanzas, 'Guilt and Sorrow; Or, Incidents on the Salisbury Plain'. At this time he very likely began to feel the insignificance of classical plot and the transcendent importance of landscape for the kind of poetry he could write. This was a recognition which, if not immediately clear from the lack of integration in 'Guilt and Sorrow', must certainly have come to him with the writing of The Borderers (1795–1797), a drama of the reign of Henry III, virtually unplayable but marvellous in its bleak moorland setting on the Scots Borders. Wordsworth said of 'Guilt and Sorrow' that 'it was addressed to coarse sympathies', probably meaning that it was an explicit attempt at narrative which failed, for he added it 'had little or no imagination about it, or invention as to story'. As he mentions in the 1842 Advertisement to the poem, Wordsworth intended to connect the histories of his two characters, a retired sailor who has committed murder and a war-impoverished woman, with the immemorial dreariness of Salisbury Plain and Stonehenge. He wanted to deal with the response of living persons to the present war, against the background of imagined wars and sufferings derived from 'the monuments and traces of antiquity, scattered in abundance over that region'. He came to Salisbury Plain (he says in the Advertisement) after a time on the Isle of Wight where he watched the British Navy massing against France; he was disturbed by war and poverty when he travelled north, but it took a specific desolate landscape to release the poem.

Coleridge saw the poem as a decisive advance in style and diction over 'Descriptive Sketches', for 'Guilt and Sorrow' occasioned the distinction in the Biographia between imagination and fancy, as well as the praise for the Wordsworthian 'fine balance of truth in observing, with the imaginative faculty in modifying, the objects observed'. Wordsworth himself, feeling the poem's plot lacked 'invention', nevertheless felt the description was 'accurate enough'. When he printed the female vagrant's tale in Lyrical Ballads (1798), he lopped off the landscape elements and the story of the retired sailor. That the two stories should have been separable does not say much for the poem's integration; yet at least the story of the guilty sailor is bound up with the bleak setting from the start and through all revisions. Already, the Wordsworthian landscape has taken on the 'visionary dreariness' of portions of *The Prelude*:

> Perplexed and comfortless he gazed around,
> And scarce could any trace of man descry,
> Save cornfields stretched and stretching without bound;
> But where the sower dwelt was nowhere to be found.
>
> . . . now along heaven's darkening cope
> The crows rushed by in eddies . . .
>   now, all wild, forlorn,
> And vacant, a huge waste around him spread.

Stonehenge is seen by the guilty runaway 'while rain poured down smoking':

> Pile of Stone-henge! so proud to hint yet keep
> Thy secrets, thou that lov'st to stand and hear
> The Plain resounding to the whirlwind's sweep,
> Inmate of lonesome Nature's endless year. . . .

As the mute observers of human waste and sacrifice, the megaliths can be invoked thus, almost as a person.

The sailor's guilty act (lacking money, he 'met a Traveller, robbed him, shed his blood': that is all the explanation offered) took place on the Plain, and so does his redemption when, encountering a father beating his son in anger, he sees the image of his crime. The sailor's sympathetic response transforms his life; he condemns his own actions but in effect he condemns all war when he says, 'within himself',

> Yet happy thou, poor boy! compared with me,
> Suffering not doing ill – fate far more mild.

Wordsworth, in a final flurry of dissatisfaction with this character and the whole poem, lets society extort full retribution by gibbeting the sailor in a public place where he is reviled by 'dissolute men': 'And to that spot . . . Women and Children were by Fathers brought'. The lurid landscape background of the gothic storm scenes, the discontinuous long stanza with its emphatic closure, the strong suggestion of the axiom that 'Suffering is permanent, obscure and dark,/ And has the nature of infinity', soon to be opposed to merely transitory 'action' in *The Borderers*, give this imperfect poem something of the quality of the 'great imaginative grotesque' as Ruskin defines it: 'A fine grotesque is the expression, in a moment, by a series of symbols thrown together in bold and fearless connection, of truths which it would have taken a long time to express in any verbal way, and of which the connection is left for the beholder to work out for himself, the gaps, left or overleaped by the haste of the imagination, forming the grotesque character.' According to Ruskin, the stern contemplation of evil and the 'tender human sympathy' of the modern grotesque have evolved a spirit of moral instruction, analogous to the effect of true gothic grotesque in the Middle Ages. The formulation applies to 'Guilt and Sorrow', a poem which despite obliquities and want of integration encounters directly the moral anomaly of murder by individual men or by nations at war. In this first poem where Wordsworth, learning how to do without straight narrative, exercises his 'original gift of spreading the tone, the *atmosphere*', there is no evasion of the guilty or sorrowing solitude of the vagrant or the alien incomprehension of earth and its monuments.

4

Coleridge's phrase 'spreading the tone' is apt. Wordsworth himself occasionally uses the same metaphor of 'spreading' in *The Prelude*, as in these remarkable lines from Book III:

> As if awakn'd, summon'd, rous'd, constrain'd,
> I look'd for universal things; perused
> The common countenance of earth and heaven;
> And, turning the mind in upon itself,
> Pored, watch'd, expected, listen'd; spread my thoughts
> And spread them with a wider creeping; felt
> Incumbences more awful, visitings
> Of the Upholder of the tranquil Soul,
> Which underneath all passion lives secure
> A steadfast life.   (1805, 11. 109–18)

Speaking of the 'common countenance of earth and heaven', Wordsworth begins by reading physiognomy into the outer landscape, modulates his discourse by 'turning the mind in', and ends by imagining an interior distance. He speaks as if he can deploy his thoughts spatially in the sort of 'landscape thinking' T. E. Hulme described as putting 'all ideas (purely mental states) into terms of *space*'. The mind extends its thoughts in an inner space with an ever 'wider creeping'; the mind has its own eye and ear and a sense of intellectual tactility which *spreads* intellection as a range of sensations within the interior distance. Within the mind, a temporal sequence of affects or thoughts is transmuted as a spread of appearances. The passage is one of several restorative moments or 'spots of time' in the poem where the mind, as Wordsworth says, shows itself 'lord and master – outward sense/The obedient servant of her will'.

But Wordsworth cannot rest purely in meditation. Luckily in such contexts the need to notice, arising in response to a felt decline in human freedom and awareness, is continually extending the self into the human and the nonhuman world. Like John Constable, his exact contemporary, Wordsworth thinks of the earth as in the deepest sense the ground of our being. Landscape poet and landscape painter share the ability to give piercing descriptions of visual, perceptual relationships; they share the premise that the modern artist's apprehension of landscape is analogous to commonplace intelligent perception. Nevertheless Wordsworth cannot so often as Constable convince himself that the nature of man is of a piece with the nature of the world in general. To the extent that landscape may be viewed as nature without man, Wordsworth recognizes that it poses a threat to mind and to life. For precisely this reason, neither can he rest purely in description. A purist descriptive poetry is an impossible ideal, though one which was essayed programmatically in Imagist poetics; for Wordsworth, such an ideal was thinkable, but nothing more.

Because he believes the descriptive and the meditative ideals must contaminate one another, there is a qualitative difference between Wordsworth's landscape poetry and that of Thomson, Gray, Cowper, and Bowles. He discovers, unravels, and actualizes possibilities which were inherent in the convention of landscape as a literary vehicle. He effects transitions between description and meditation, plausible ways of blending the aesthetic and the ethical modes of the mind within the process of a single poem. His wish to 'spread' his thoughts and 'spread them with a wider creeping' unites a conception of the outer scene with a wide range of inner sensations, pervading description with thought and giving speculation a local habitation and a name. If, as I believe, there is a relation between Wordsworth's very syntax and his preoccupation with landscape, then we must take seriously his deliberate verb 'spread' and its cognate words. At best, the fascination with landscape and the love for open, meditative forms are integral in his poetry: as he spreads his attention, whether outwards in description or inwards in meditation, so he spreads his poems by the extension of syntax in blank verse.

A word like 'spread' carries over its literal, palpable sense of materiality into primarily idealist or mystical contexts. Similarly, Wordsworth uses the words 'thing' and 'thought' to much effect, for there is always some of the aura, the residue, of the meaning of the one when the other word is employed. The two are sometimes in every respect interchangeable:

> A motion and a spirit, that impels
> All thinking things, all objects of all thought,
> And rolls through all things.

> ('Tintern Abbey')

A growing reverence for the literal, we imagine, forced Wordsworth's rejection of Hartleian mechanical association in favour of the 'streamy nature of association'; the hope was that the Augustan disciplines of logic and rhetoric, and the image-making powers of the landscape genre, should have an equally important part to play in the creation of poetry. Often the results in poems were idiosyncratic or merely silly; but the effectiveness of the general programme may be suggested in one particular, the masterful legerdemain of the connective and assertive 'Hence', 'Thus', 'So' in the best of Wordsworth, which so often act as compelling transitions after a description, turning observations into arguments in the absence of explicit dialectic.

The tendency of Wordsworth in his frequent confusions about the status of language – now a set of dead moulds, now the locus of the actual world – and of Coleridge in his studies of great poets, was to assimilate nature to poetry, poetry to nature. The relation between poetry and nature seen concretely in textures and forms had never been so close. In *The Friend* (1810) Coleridge writes:

> If in Shakespeare we find nature idealised into poetry,
> through the creative power of a profound yet observant
> meditation, so through the meditative observation of a
> Davy, a Woolaston, of a Hatchett, –
> > By some connatural force,
> > Powerful at greatest distance to unify
> > With secret amity things of like kind,

we find poetry, as it were, substantiated and realised in nature; yea, nature itself disclosed to us, *geminam istam naturam, quae fit et facit, et creat et creatur*, as at once the poet and the poem.

The poem as part of nature, part of creation yet creating too, meant the interpenetration of consciousness and its objects. 'Meditative observation', a term used here for three scientists and Shakespeare, was used later, in the *Biographia*, for Wordsworth himself, when Coleridge describes the 'weight and sanity' of Wordsworth's thoughts, 'won, not from books; but from the poet's own meditative observation. They are fresh and have the dew upon them'. This denial of dualism had in fact a sophisticated series of checks on itself: not least in the unobtrusive concessive phrases like 'as if' and 'somehow' which show how any specific attribution of thought to object is conscious, qualified, and heuristic. Most significant, of course, is the wide range of landscape effects – of mist, distance, optical illusion, colouring, perspective, and the like – which by their very particularity resist idealization almost successfully and remain alien and external. To Wordsworth and Coleridge, following the eighteenth-century ideas of order, Nature may be said to possess her own aesthetic media, whose change and diversity will – when well noticed – be strong proof that a world exists outside the registering mind.

The union of observation and meditation is clearly explained by Coleridge when he says sensation is intelligence itself revealed as an earlier power in the process of self-construction. That is, we do not learn to have concepts but to differentiate them. The order of a poetry on these premises will be epistemological, the issues personal. Such a poetry will tend to hover and eddy, to remain with experience trying to get behind and around it, as it were, to extort the full personal significance; no more, but certainly no less. The order, again, will trace the lines from nascent vision to full critical intelligence in separate encounters of mind and world which in a larger context stand as analogies for personal growth. 'The Growth of a Poet's Mind' will be a typical outer frame, as will the image of a river or brook. Coleridge, considering that in Cowper's *Task* the connections were 'frequently awkward, and the transitions abrupt and arbitrary', sought for a subject which would provide ordonnance: 'a subject, that should give equal room and freedom for description, incident, and impassioned reflections on man, nature, and society, yet supply in itself a natural connection to the parts, and unity to the whole. Such a subject I conceived myself to have found in a stream, traced from its source in the hills.' Consciousness and the stream or breeze which is its analogue make the maximum poetic demand for continuity and transition; the bias of the eighteenth century in favour of design is held in abeyance, and the impulse to straight narrative is controverted.

Eighteenth-century poets with the exception of Cowper had used psychological expressions independently of personal pronouns. With the transition to Romanticism, images of stream and wind-harp began to imply that the created poem was most fully part of nature when the poet was himself both author and subject, and the use of personal pronouns became closely related to the language of things. Characteristically, Wordsworth admitted of *The Prelude* that it was 'a thing unprecedented in literary history that a man should talk so much about himself'. To the extent that *The Prelude* applies concepts to images and tests concepts and predilections by perceptual encounter, it may be called one man's full attempt to understand the world. Though its outer framework may suggest causal connections of plot, the poem is not properly a narrative possessing the attributes of sequence and verisimilitude. 'This meditative History', as Wordsworth calls it, is rather a poem of remembered and therefore managed landscapes along with ideas generated at the time of writing, which dares to be digressive, disintegrative, as it knows it cannot be conceived or written at one sitting. In this context, however, a 'managed landscape' cannot rightly mean a landscape controlled or fully formulated; the interest of many passages is often in the degree of difference between the formulation which is offered and the hopes and fears actually enacted in the landscape description.

As the only factors of order and coherence strictly necessary, Wordsworth believes in the availability of certain trains of association with their multiple moral interconnections, and in the 'more than usual organic sensibility' of himself the protagonist. Without the meditative generalization which surrounds and acclimatizes the 'spots of time' the poem would not have been written; like the blank verse medium, at once weighty and fluid, such generalization provides a common routine home for extraordinary vision, balancing Rhetoric and Poetic in the same poem. Wordsworth printed a few segments of the poem separately, but must himself have seen how difficult it was to represent the whole by anything less than itself: *The Prelude* must be read entire as a mind rehearsing itself.

5

The triumph of such organization is of course *The Prelude's* satellite poem, 'Tintern Abbey'. According to Max J. Friedländer, in the history of landscape painting artists appear to observe sharply single parts of scenes without being able to give verisimilitude to a whole composition which relates parts to one another; isolated parts are accumulated, 'until, in the last phase the particular segment is approached from some vantage point or other and all the details are arranged according to space-logic' (*Landscape, Portrait, Still-Life*, 1949). Wordsworth takes himself through a similar development in the 1790s between 'Descriptive Sketches' and 'Tintern Abbey', the latter a poem which uses a straightforward first person singular mode of address and a specifically announced vantage 'Here, under this dark sycamore'. Better than the couplets and stanzas of the early descriptive poems, blank verse preserves the ebb and sway of emotional pressure and blends sentence and section with little sense of formal division.

In fact, the achievement of various sorts of blendings – of observations and mental states into one another, and of progressive transition in the verse itself – is this poem's way of enacting habits of meditation. The outer landscape, important in itself and as a reminder of the Wordsworth who visited the Wye Valley five years before, is observed yet curiously transparent. The vividly noticed details of cliffs and valley, cottages, orchards, woodlands, 'wreaths of smoke', perhaps especially the unseen imagined Hermit who poet-like 'sits alone', are all wonderfully noticed, yet they are also phenomena of the mind and images of rural meditation. The steep protective cliffs 'impress' on the 'wild secluded scene. . . . Thoughts of more deep seclusion', and these thoughts are the poem itself. So secluded is the scene that the smoke wreaths which imply human presence ascend undispersed 'in silence, from among the trees'.

Now if, as is likely, Wordsworth had with him William Gilpin's *Tour of the Wye* (1771) as a reference and guide, he could have found there descriptions of a setting 'sequestered from the commerce of life' profoundly amenable to his passion for solitude. Gilpin begins his description of the Valley by contrasting it with Monmouth Castle farther up the Wye: 'The castle, meant for defence, stands boldly on the hill: the abbey, intended for meditation, is hid in the sequestered vale', surrounded by the summits of hills 'which include the whole', and 'leave no room for inclement blasts to enter'. By blunting 'the sharp edges of the chissel [sic]' and taking possession of the walls by ivy and lichens, 'the ornaments of time', Nature has now made the ruin of Tintern 'her own'. The affinities with Gilpin persist through the first twenty-two descriptive lines of the poem. In the rest of the poem Wordsworth searches to the bottom the implications of Gilpin's method and the method of loco-descriptive poetry. It is Wordsworth's emphasis on seclusion as the precondition of mature human thought, inseparable from the opening lines of apparent description, which unites the opening of the poem with the solemn thinking which follows. With what Coleridge called 'the rapidity necessary to Pathos', it prepares the effortless transition to another phase of the subject, the notions of absence and ecstasy in the second verse-paragraph. By a masterful act of premeditation or 'composition', imagination presents the whole poem in the opposition of exposure and seclusion, absence and return, in the opening landscape.

The tentative, exploratory thinking in the body of 'Tintern Abbey' moves through a process of intellection which deepens the reference of the opening description: the poem becomes the perfect flowering of the loco-descriptive genre. The distinction of Wordsworth is that at best landscape is inseparable from such sequences of generalization. 'There is also a meditative, as well as a human, pathos,' he said, 'an enthusiastic, as well as an ordinary, sorrow; a sadness that has its seat in the depths of reason, to which the mind cannot sink gently of itself – but to which it must descend by treading the steps of thought' (*PW*, II, 428). Here is a passage from the heart of the poem in the central meditative style:

> And now, with gleams of half-extinguished thought,
> With many recognitions dim and faint,
> And somewhat of a sad perplexity,
> The picture of the mind revives again:
> While here I stand, not only with the sense
> Of present pleasure, but with pleasing thoughts
> That in this moment there is life and food
> For future years. And so I dare to hope,
> Though changed, no doubt, from what I was when first
> I came among these hills; when like a roe
> I bounded o'er the mountains, by the sides
> Of the deep rivers, and the lonely streams,

23

C

Wherever nature led: more like a man
Flying from something that he dreads than one
Who sought the thing he loved. For nature then
(The coarser pleasures of my boyish days,
And their glad animal movements all gone by)
To me was all in all. – I cannot paint
What then I was. The sounding cataract
Haunted me like a passion: the tall rock,
The mountain, and the deep and gloomy wood,
Their colours and their forms, were then to me
An appetite; a feeling and a love,
That had no need of a remoter charm,
By thought supplied, nor any interest
Unborrowed from the eye.

The passage acquaints us with a mind almost entirely in possession
of its experience. The noble and declarative language moves with
tough intent towards the actualizing of that experience and the discovery of its personal meaning and use. There is no need for symbol,
though 'the sounding cataract' and 'An appetite' do seem to imply
something more than literal fact. Instead the style might be called
excursive or generative; clauses are linked by association, and sen-
tences carry the discourse further by a simple 'And so' or 'For'; indeed the connective 'and' is worked hard, as is the amplifying 'not
only . . . but' construction. The back-and-forth movement from past
to present time, the intrusive present consciousness qualifying nos-
talgia at every point as soon as it is expressed, the very convolutions
of tense, re-enact the processes of a mind in the throes of self-defini-
tion.

Wordsworth continues:

– That time is past,
And all its aching joys are now no more,
And all its dizzy raptures. Not for this
Faint I, nor mourn nor murmur; other gifts
Have followed; for such loss, I would believe,
Abundant recompense. For I have learned
To look on nature, not as in the hour
Of thoughtless youth; but hearing oftentimes
The still, sad music of humanity,
Nor harsh nor grating, though of ample power
To chasten and subdue. And I have felt

A presence that disturbs me with the joy
Of elevated thoughts; a sense sublime
Of something far more deeply interfused,
Whose dwelling is the light of setting suns,
And the round ocean and the living air,
And the blue sky, and in the mind of man:
A motion and a spirit, that impels
All thinking things, all objects of all thought,
And rolls through all things. Therefore am I still
A lover of the meadows and the woods,
And mountains; and of all that we behold
From this green earth; of all the mighty world
Of eye, and ear, – both what they half create,
And what perceive; well pleased to recognise
In nature and the language of the sense
The anchor of my purest thoughts, the nurse,
The guide, the guardian of my heart, and soul
Of all my mortal being.

We are convinced, carried onward by the authenticity of such a mind
when it is so engaged, and we come to know what Wordsworth
means when he says the purpose of his poems 'is to follow the fluxes
and refluxes of the mind when agitated by the great and simple affections of our nature'. We also understand his notion that in this kind
of writing even 'repetition and apparent tautology are frequently
beauties of the highest kind' (*PW*, II, 388 n, 513). As a 'highly imaginative' poem – unlike those of his poems he called 'simply human' –
'Tintern Abbey' is in conception allowably dishevelled, tautological,
irregular. For although Wordsworth makes a show of ratiocination,
it can hardly be said that he is here following the steps of an argument. Rather, his method is to exhibit the complete movement of a
full mind which has found a pretext for its own examination: a
mapping of the self with relation to a significant landscape.

Dr. Johnson's criticism of the 'great defect' of Thomson's *Seasons* as
a lack of 'method' applies, for Wordworth, writing a poem similar to
Thomson's in its descriptive-meditative intent, manages to avoid
the haphazard construction of the earlier poem: by designing a continuity: by arranging the gradual revelation of a discovery: or, to
put it another way, by moving steadily deeper into his subject. Em-
phasizing movement and continuity, Wordsworth once remarked
that the poem 'was written with a hope that in the transitions, and the

impassioned music of the versification', would be found the impet-
uosity he thought characteristic of the Ode form (PW, II, 517). On
the level of the line, the achieved meditative style is amplifying, incremental. Wordsworth's strength is that of plain syntax: meaning
draped over the ends of blank-verse lines, most often pulled up short
at line-end; or back-tracking, eliding past punctuation marks, creating and destroying balance in the phrasing. Parallelism ('with gleams
. . . with many recognitions'), apposition, digressive delay, inversion
('recognitions dim'), parataxis, polysyndeton ('And the round ocean
and the living air,/And the blue sky'), negative affirmation ('nor any
interest/Unborrowed from the eye') – the list covers only a few of the
major elements of a discourse which rarely lets thought cling to a
metaphor, preferring to 'spread' it by extension of syntax. The final
ten-line sentence of this passage affords an instance: a masterful use
of the connective 'and' keeps syntax lucid, telescoping or expanding
the sense as required, contributing to the density of 'both what they
half create,/And what perceive'.

The use of the transitional (but not strictly logical) 'Therefore' is
one of the stylistic habits of the poem as a whole – as is the bold
dash, the intensifying 'all' or 'purest', and the catalogue whose mem-
bers ascend in significance. One catalogue has the device we may call
'faulty series':

> . . . something far more deeply interfused,
> Whose dwelling is the light of setting suns,
> And the round ocean and the living air,
> And the blue sky, and in the mind of man . . .

The preposition 'in' complicates the progression, bearing as it does
the full weight of Wordsworthian pondering on mind and world.
The calculated vagueness of 'something' may seem an evasion, like
the anxious circumlocution near the end of the poem, 'If I should be
where I no more can hear/Thy voice', where Wordsworth seems to
imply his death. We can speculate that he uses vagueness or peri-
phrasis to get over gaps, to touch only lightly on matters about which
he is uncertain. Occasionally he gives an honest admission – 'I cannot
paint/What then I was' – which aids the illusion of spontaneity: the
poem as the act of the mind, finding its own materials, brooding on
its habitual associations, admitting limits.

This is an impression reinforced by the blank-verse lines, which
in every way deny closure and pause. All but the first sentence in
these passages begins in mid-line; sense thrusts from caesura to

caesura, not from line to line, giving the poem a suppleness which
the blank verse of Akenside or Young – trapped in Miltonic rhythms
– could not manage. In some cases, the rhythms of the poem operate
all but independently of punctuation. Wordsworth has a habit of
seeming to conclude a thought with an exclamation point or a fairly
decisive close (as for instance the ';—'), and then moving past the
punctuation with a new parallel or correlative phrase or series of
phrases. To select one of many possible examples, we may note the
transition in lines 18–19, where he pushes past the exclamation point
to add a new and related series of lines which make sense only when
read in the light of what has come before. Possibly this habit derives
in part from oral composition: 'I began [the poem] upon leaving
Tintern,' Wordsworth says, 'and concluded it just as I was entering
Bristol.' His own interest in the transitions and music of the poem
may well owe something to these circumstances; and obviously the
punctuation was supplied later during transcription. The poem has
only the blank-verse line to keep it pent-in, and the continuous discourse could be rehearsed, expanded, kept in mind all at once up to
any given point – as even a slightly longer poem could not. During
that 'ramble of four or five days', the moral and personal significance
of a perceptual event could be explored, and all the relevant areas of
the mind engaged. The poem would thus be a movement of meditation as the result of a difficult, unsettling perception of the difference
between a changing self and an unchanging landscape.

One result would be a language for the expression of an intense
inwardness, which would at the same time be a language which could
deal descriptively with the external world. The process of meditative
observation, aided by a special, repeating vocabulary equivocal in its
blending of thought into thing, distinguishes this poem from all
eighteenth-century poems which – in practice if not in principle –
tended to separate the descriptive from the meditative modes. Wordsworth uses 'more' and 'deep' (to pick only two instances) at nearly
every point of emotional elevation, particularly where their ambiguity would deflect any pressure of examination or contradiction:
'Thoughts of more deep seclusion'; 'something far more deeply interfused'.

Another, more central result would be a language, partly personal
in connotation, which contained a sufficiently large but fixed number
of words as movable counters for use in amplifying and illuminating
different contexts. For 'Tintern Abbey' contains not only the syntacti-
cal repetitions-with-change mentioned above, but an extraordinarily

repetitive vocabulary. To take one instance, the word 'landscape', occurring at the beginning of the poem (1. 24) and in the
second-last line, cannot be arbitrary in its placement as one of many
elements bringing the discourse back to 'those steep woods and lofty
cliffs' and a more literal reality at the close – where the poet, but for
the reflective middle of the poem, ends as he began. The effect of repeating other words as well – 'murmur', 'impress', 'wild', 'behold',
'eye', 'heart', 'form(s)', 'live' – is to deepen and extend a notion
already stated: to make 'impassioned music' from the discursive and
naked language of the thinking mind.

There is, then, a connection between meditative style and the
poem's intent of weighing the 'aching joys' of 'thoughtless youth'
against an adult's consciousness which is no longer naïve about perception. For even in the opening landscape Wordsworth is 'spreading
the tone . . . of the ideal world around forms', selecting and trans-
muting his details with delicate concern, attending to transitions,
deepening key words in their contexts. There is no essential division
between the first and second verse-paragraphs, merely the modulation
of a discourse which from the start – to borrow two phrases from
Coleridge – sets about 'reducing multitude into unity of effect' ('clad
in one green hue') by the action of 'meditative observation' (hedge-
rows become 'little lines/Of sportive wood run wild' by such seeing).
There is some straining when Wordsworth states that his gain equals
his loss; and his final words to Dorothy, 'Nor wilt thou then forget'
(11. 155 f.), are not so much a statement as an anxious plea. Yet the
impressive final sentence of the verse-paragraph quoted, where he
asserts a new morality of perception with 'nature and the language of
the sense' as 'soul/Of all my moral being', does much to convince us
that his assertion is plausible; as does the poem's last line, with its
careful reference to the language of interfusion which so clearly asso-
ciates spirit with its setting in the objective landscape. Carried along
by the continuity of the poem are contradictory elements of the sort
that are united in actual experience but dissolve upon merely logical
inspection: the 'mysticism' of the poem ('we see into the life of
things') corrects itself by the inclusion of specifics; orotund abstraction by description or the plain style ('that best portion of a good
man's life'); and the inward preoccupation of the adult mind, by
continual acknowledgement of the educative value of landscape.

Brilliantly, Keats realized the achievement of the poem, calling it a
proof Wordsworth could 'think into the human heart', a poem with
no attained 'balance of good and evil' yet 'explorative of those dark

passages' of responsible life reached at the brink of maturity. The wonder of the poem – certainly vital for informing our sense of Wordsworthian style in its broadest definition – is that such a capacious utterance could have been written during a casual ramble, 'the last twenty lines or so being composed as he walked down the hill from Clifton to Bristol' (see *PW*, II, 517).

2
Images of exposure

I

One way of reading 'Tintern Abbey' is as a dialectic between exposure and seclusion, between youthful receptivity to experience and the mature man's tendency to formulate experience. The same holds true for many poems of Wordsworth's late twenties and his thirties. After 1798, his decision to write a poem on his own mind is, as he says, a safer, less demanding task than the philosophical poem on man, nature, and human life, for which he claims to be preparing. In *The Prelude*, only indirectly is the subject man in his relation to the human community; that is the theme of the unwritten *Recluse*. In this sense, at least, *The Prelude* is a neophyte's poem, and as such preparatory, prudential. A. J. Ayer in *The Problem of Knowledge* (1961) discusses the need for personal security implicit in a fascination with sheer being:

> Statements which do no more than describe the content of a momentary, private experience achieve the greatest security because they run the smallest risk. But they do run some risk, however small, and because of this they too can come to grief. Complete security is attained only by statements like 'I exist' which function as gesticulations. But the price which they pay for it is a sacrifice of descriptive content.

This puts one in mind of the privacy of meditative poems like 'Tintern Abbey' and *The Prelude*, which are nominally addressed to an audience of one and deal ostensibly with the transactions of one man's mind with the particular landscapes of a corner of England.

In such poems Wordsworth is to be traced at his best when he is putting checks on the inordinate desire for complete security: when he risks the qualification of inner by outer reality, when he risks the qualification of programmatic meditation by description. In the second half of *The Prelude*, when he turns from experiences of educative landscape to an external narrative of events in London and revolutionary France, he is speaking in a context of diminished risk. He has come far from that dangerous freedom, dramatized in the poem's opening lines, which is the source of the metaphysical images of exposure – prospect, excursion, solitary wanderer, desolate landscape – at the very centre of his achievement.

For Wordsworth, only the imagery of natural forms is genuine; only landscape imagery is truly imaginative. Once poetry began to enlist perspective, distance, texture, effects of light, visual illusion and the like painterly effects it became, by degrees in the last half of the eighteenth century, of necessity autobiographical. By the time 'Tintern Abbey' was written, authenticity required that the perceiver be placed in a landscape poem, and the first person pronoun was becoming the norm. The poetic diction of neo-classic nature poetry, an attempt to give an appropriate degree of description by importing epithets and structures from Latin and terms from science, was all but obsolete and was to receive its death blow in Wordsworth's 1800 Preface to *Lyrical Ballads*. Like his contemporaries Turner and Constable, Wordsworth aimed at the elimination of all conflicting imagery save that of landscape. Wild and semi-wild scenery became that body of images in which Nature as an ideal was represented. In effect, landscape was a strategic reduction of the idea of nature.

Though the most revealing stylistic unit in all Romantic landscape poets is the image, in the case of Wordsworth it is not precise to speak of images as in any usual way symbolic. Wordsworth dated from age fourteen his resolution to supply the deficiency in poetry of noticing 'the infinite variety of natural appearances', and he defined imagery in a highly nominalist manner as 'sensible objects really existing, and felt to exist', which 'may form the materials of a descriptive poem, where objects are delineated as they are'. In poetry, his way of showing wordless unity with the forms of nature would be to say of the child, 'the visible scene/Would enter unawares into his mind/With all its solemn imagery'.

When imagery is oftentimes considered not as formal conceit but as the living locus of descriptive poems in the external world, the non-metaphorical and unwitty poetry which results will, often uncritically, take physical for spiritual as a matter of course and will often complain that the outer senses exert a tyranny over the mind. Wordsworth demanded a great deal of language. He believed it would under certain conditions of grace permit an adult artist to reproduce the unified conditions of childhood consciousness, and to implement this he developed – in the midst of a more formal rhetoric – a reasonably extensive set of terms for speaking simultaneously of physical and spiritual happenings. Wordsworth contrasted 'the imaginative influences which I have endeavoured to throw over common life' in his poem 'Lucy Gray' with 'Crabbe's matter of fact style of treating subjects of the same kind'. His criticism of Scott, that 'what he writes in the way of natural description is merely rhyming nonsense' because he never gets beneath the surface of things, is to the point:

> S[cott] . . . confounds *imagery* with *imagination*. Sensible objects really existing, and felt to exist are imagery; and they may form the materials of a descriptive poem, where objects are delineated as they are. Imagination is a subjective term: it deals with objects not as they are, but as they appear to the mind of the poet.
>
> The imagination is that intellectual lens through the medium of which the poetical observer sees the objects of his observation, modified both in form and colour

and with discordant elements blended into the comprehensive impression (*Memoirs*, 1851, II, 447). His early rejection of the methods of picturesque noticing and straight narrative was due to a progressive acknowledgement of habits of meditation which were directly consequent to an exercise of that 'art of seeing' he found wanting in the poetry between *Paradise Lost* and *The Seasons*. In his new mode, as he says, 'the feeling . . . developed gives importance to the action and situation, and not the action and situation to the feeling'; thus plot is reduced to autobiography, nature to local landscape.

For Wordsworth, an instinctive adherence to the method of premeditating, of grasping the emotional key of the whole in imagination, meant a steadily deepening power of images from nature in the decade between 'Descriptive Sketches' and 'Resolution and Independence'. At the same time, as this chapter is intended to show, change and death in the peopled landscape draw his increasing attention. Wordsworth would not reprint 'Descriptive Sketches' until 1849; but 'Resolution and Independence', with its magnificent images of stone, sea-beast, and cloud, became his leading instance how 'the conferring, the abstracting, and the modifying powers of the imagination, immediately and mediately acting, are all brought into conjunction'. Often in this period, he speaks of objects apprehended not as they are, but as they appear to the mind of the poet, as the sustenance or food of the mind, with memory the implied process of digestion, incorporation, nurture. The verbs feed, nourish, nurse, spread, circumfuse, espouse, indicate spiritual analogies derived from purely physical acts.

Once such analogies have been advanced it is but a short step to belief in the educative value of the forms of nature. And it is easiest and most appropriate to believe this of the child:

> Wisdom and Spirit of the universe!
> Thou Soul that art the Eternity of Thought!
> That giv'st to forms and images a breath
> And everlasting motion! not in vain,
> By day or star-light thus from my first dawn
> Of Childhood didst Thou intertwine for me
> The passions that build up our human Soul,
> Not with the mean and vulgar works of Man,
> But with high objects, with enduring things,
> With life and nature, purifying thus
> The elements of feeling and of thought,
> And sanctifying, by such discipline,
> Both pain and fear, until we recognize
> A grandeur in the beatings of the heart.

> (1805, I, 11. 428–41)

For the child, sensation is itself a form of thinking and learning. The child is not yet obliged to encounter 'the mean and vulgar works of Man': 'enduring things' are his teachers and they are the 'Ministers' of nature and life. All that is required is that he be open to experience. For the mature poet, the paradox of such openness and exposure is that, while it is the condition of experiencing and the ground of vision, it runs counter to any settled habits of meditation; such habits must be revised at every perceptual encounter. The retrospective poet will prize meditative seclusion and unique transcendental 'spots of time' because he prefers to remain with the formative experience instead of submitting himself to the undifferentiated flow of sensation.

The very earliest of Wordsworth's poems, slightly under the sway of the fashionable melancholy in vogue after the 'graveyard school' of poets, connect exposure with activity of the senses and seclusion with a prized condition of vacant stillness. In the first of the Poems Written in Youth (1787), he imagines the 'longing look' he will cast back on his native regions after a journey away from home – an entirely characteristic forecast which sets 'local sympathy' counter to the wandering impulse at a time when he could have no knowledge whatever of his life after school. The second poem of this group, with its kinetic first line, puts the contrary impulses into a genuine landscape setting:

> Calm is all nature as a resting wheel.
> The kine are couched upon the dewy grass;
> The horse alone, seen dimly as I pass,
> Is cropping audibly his later meal:
> Dark is the ground; a slumber seems to steal
> O'er vale, and mountain, and the starless sky.
> Now, in this blank of things, a harmony,
> Home-felt, and home-created, comes to heal
> That grief for which the senses still supply
> Fresh food; for only then, when memory
> Is hushed, am I at rest. My Friends! restrain
> Those busy cares that would allay my pain;
> Oh! leave me to myself, nor let me feel
> The officious touch that makes me droop again.

The darkening pastoral landscape – a 'blank of things' where objects are stripped of their utilitarian association by twilight – is the container whose stillness the speaker wishes to share by anaesthetizing or starving his senses. His desire is to be the kind of agent that is at one with this kind of scene; alive yet in a solitary stasis, without memory like the wheel or like the single horse which can eat without feeding grief. Without its first six lines of ingenuous description the poem would hardly be impressive as a plea for escape from vulnerable grief. The chosen details, all in key, arrested and idealized, authenticate the wish *not to be touched* which ends the poem. As scene requires agent, images of seclusion require images of exposure for their dialectical counterpart.

A late fragment, 'Airey-Force Valley' (1835), prizes stillness too. But, finding it even more delightful when there is slight animation, the poem arranges contrasting stillness and motion into concert. In the opening description, trees in the sequestered valley glen, untouched by 'boisterous winds that rage without', are 'steadfast as the rocks'; even the moving brook 'Doth rather deepen than disturb the calm'. And yet, even now, Wordsworth continues, a little breeze

> Has entered, by the sturdy oaks unfelt,
> But to its gentle touch how sensitive
> Is the light ash! that, pendent from the brow

Of yon dim cave, in seeming silence makes
A soft eye-music of slow-waving boughs,
Powerful almost as vocal harmony
To stay the wanderer's steps and soothe his thoughts.

Half a century after 'Calm is all nature as a resting wheel', Wordsworth is still employing the trope of 'touch' as an image of exposure,
and turning nature into an object of aesthetic speculation. But it is a
more vital 'harmony' this time, for oaks can perhaps feel, the ash is
sensitive, the cave has a brow, a tree makes silent eye-music. Along
with an equal delight in the ways oaks and ash take the breeze,
Wordsworth reads physiognomy in the forms of nature, nuancing
and authenticating his attributions by such unobtrusive qualifications as 'seeming' and 'almost', and by providing an individual observer who is moved by the scene. It is enough to entrance
any wanderer when the world thus organizes itself into poem or
song.

Far more frequently, however, nature will resist formulation and
seem to assert its otherness and intractability, invading even the
places of deepest seclusion. In the first book of The Prelude, Wordsworth uses the rhetoric of fancy to describe 'Our home-amusements
by the warm peat fire' during winter evenings, the games of tic-tac-
toe, loo, or whist in the cottages of his childhood:

Oh, with what echoes on the board they fell!
Ironic diamonds, – clubs, hearts, diamonds, spades,
A congregation piteously akin!

And so on. But the passage ends with a shift to the outside world:

Meanwhile abroad
Incessant rain was falling, or the frost
Raged bitterly, with keen and silent tooth;
And, interrupting oft that eager game,
From under Esthwaite's splitting fields of ice
The pent-up air, struggling to free itself,
Gave out to meadow grounds and hills a loud
Protracted yelling, like the noise of wolves
Howling in troops along the Bothnic Main.

(11. 535–43)

With the same abrupt notation 'meanwhile', indicating not transition but utter disjunction from the ordinary boyish routine, the
universe 'not unnoticed' obtrudes its mysterious comment on the
skaters and their din.

     – All shod with steel,
We hiss'd along the polish'd ice, in games
Confederate, imitative of the chace
And woodland pleasures, the resounding horn,
The Pack loud bellowing, and the hunted hare.
So through the darkness and the cold we flew,
And not a voice was idle; with the din,
Meanwhile, the precipices rang aloud,
The leafless trees, and every icy crag
Tinkled like iron, while the distant hills
Into the tumult sent an alien sound
Of melancholy, not unnoticed, while the stars,
Eastward, were sparkling clear, and in the west
The orange sky of evening died away.

                                          (1805, I, 11. 460–73)

Sounds sent out joyous and human are echoed back alien, melancholy. Here as above the delight of the game is not obliterated, but qualified, perhaps heightened, by 'other modes of being' which exist as the permanent ground of common perception and social life.

2

Unless he now confounds his present being with the past, Wordsworth says in 'Nutting', 'even then . . . I felt a sense of pain'. An under-sense of the artifice and fragility of the merely social world, its frequent contradiction by an alien dispensation, haunts Wordsworth's scenes of visionary exposure on waste moor or open road, mountain or ocean. It informs his apocalyptic dream of the wanderer figure, the Arab-Quixote 'hurrying o'er the illimitable waste/With the fleet waters of a drowning world/In chase of him' (*Prelude*, V). And, as I have suggested, exposure is the implied subject of Book I of *The Prelude*, where with the courage of his confusion Wordsworth shows the dangerous freedom of the landscape poet stranded in nature without a theme. In the first lines of the long poem, Wordsworth declares his release 'from yon City's walls . . . A prison where he hath been long immured', and states that the burden of his 'unnatural self' is 'shaken off'. He then writes one of the most curiously confessional introductions in all literature when he proceeds from this presumably spontaneous declaration of freedom to a rehearsal of his powers and a listing of possible topics for long poems – all the chosen topics centring on the idea of a heroic political liberty which unconsciously mirrors his literary quandary.

'A subtle selfishness,' he says, 'doth lock my functions up in blank reserve'. The difficulty he describes is that of the mind which can do nothing with the manifold of sensation, craving a link with history yet finding everything, or nothing, significant:

> – Ah! better far than this, to stray about
> Voluptuously through fields and rural walks,
> And ask no record of the hours, given up
> To vacant musing, unreprov'd neglect
> Of all things, and deliberate holiday. . . .
>
> (1805, I, 11. 252–6)

But 'deliberate holiday' is exactly, in a phrase, the perplexity. A turn to gentle reverence in the verse when he invokes the memory of the River Derwent and his childhood in itself announces that he has found his subject:

> Was it for this
> That one, the fairest of all Rivers, lov'd
> To blend his murmurs with my Nurse's song,
> And from his alder shades and rocky falls,
> And from his fords and shallows, sent a voice
> That flow'd along my dreams?

The river, he says, 'composed' his thoughts when he was a child; so it does here too when he is a man and an artist, leading him to himself as the most promising poetic subject. The 271 lines preceding this question were in fact supplied as a beginning in 1803. Thus the whole introduction of the poem, with its naked confessional exposure, was invented to provide a rationale for the collection of landscape fragments with bridge-passages which dated from 1798–9. The true solution to the question of a subject put in the opening lines becomes, in the version of 1805, the poem as a whole in thirteen books.

The first lines of The Prelude describe, in terms of the art of writing, a perplexity of experience generally. This contradictory joy and threat of exposure is to be found in its purest form in those same discontinuous instances of tutorial by landscape, now the best parts of Books I and II, for which Wordsworth was ex post facto providing con-

text and introduction by applying the frame of an autobiographical
poem addressed to Coleridge. 'Fair seed-time had my soul, and I grew
up/Foster'd by beauty and by fear': the beauty and pleasure bound
up with the fear in these tutorial episodes is specifically conceived as
aesthetic, an interplay and blending of the sublime and beautiful.
Wordsworth in this emphasis makes it impossible for his readers to
forget that his is a narrative of the growth of a poet's mind. This premise controls and masters the details even where not obviously the
case, and verisimilitude in dating and circumstance does not matter
so much as truth to the formative process of the experience. At the
beginning or end of each episode is a brief but explicit discursive
statement, explaining the purpose of its inclusion. By starting the
series with three occasions of boyhood theft (Book I, 1. 309 f.),
Wordsworth in the most impressive way demonstrates the texture of
childhood consciousness in its response to the ethical promptings of
the natural world. The landscape poetry that results is at once descriptive and meditative, aesthetic and ethical in its substance.

'Though mean/My object, and inglorious, yet the end/Was not
ignoble': if he had not attempted such violation, and dared exposure,
he would not have received a poet's instruction by 'Severer interven-
tions, ministry/More palpable'. Along with the following episode,
the near-by incidents of snare-plundering and boat-stealing are perhaps the best examples in Wordsworthian landscape of a directly
ethical treatment of the relations of scene and agent:

> Oh! when I have hung
> Above the raven's nest, by knots of grass
> And half-inch fissures in the slippery rock
> But ill-sustained, and almost (so it seemed)
> Suspended by the blast that blew amain,
> Shouldering the naked crag, oh, at that time
> While on the perilous ridge I hung alone,
> With what strange utterance did the loud dry wind
> Blow through my ear! the sky seemed not a sky
> Of earth – and with what motion moved the clouds!
>
> (I, 11. 330–39)

Wordsworth discusses 'hung' in his 1815 Preface as a verb expressing imaginative energy: here it achieves the almost visceral quality
of danger at the end of an enjambing line, and like 'seemed', 'Oh' and
the passionate exclamation point is used more than once with effect
in very few lines. The boy is supported and threatened at once and by

38

the same elements of wind and rock; his peril teaches by bringing access of untellable knowledge and power, keener because of the threat involved.

The wonderful allegation that the wind blew 'threw my ears' illustrates how thoroughly these moments interpenetrate inner with outer while preserving their intrinsic differences. Wordsworth shows the mind not so much open to experience as literally in the midst of it. This fusion of thing and concept makes for the queer literalness of the Wordsworthian image, apparent also in the phrase 'given our bodies to the wind' in the description of ice-skating:

> Not seldom from the uproar I retired
> Into a silent bay, or sportively
> Glanced sideway, leaving the tumultuous throng,
> To cut across the reflex of a star
> That fled, and, flying still before me, gleamed
> Upon the glassy plain; and oftentimes,
> When we had given our bodies to the wind,
> And all the shadowy banks on either side
> Came sweeping through the darkness, spinning still
> The rapid line of motion, then at once
> Have I, reclining back upon my heels,
> Stopped short; yet still the solitary cliffs
> Wheeled by me – even as if the earth had rolled
> With visible motion her diurnal round!
> Behind me did they stretch in solemn train,
> Feebler and feebler, and I stood and watched
> Till all was tranquil as a dreamless sleep.
>
> (I, 11. 447–63)

This was the passage which Coleridge in The Friend (December, 1810) quoted with its introductory materials under Wordsworth's title 'Growth of Genius From the Influence of Natural Objects on the Imagination, in Boyhood and Youth'. Two momentary separations from the gregarious band of skaters produce deepening intuitions of the strangeness of the world. Just as on 'the naked crag' the sky 'seemed not a sky/Of earth', the earth here is seen to accelerate its motion, caught out in its seemingly sympathetic revolutions when the poet 'at once . . . Stopped short'.

'A dreamless sleep' is imageless. The imagination is pictured as so gorged by the chance gift of insight into the workings of the world that though Wordsworth 'stood and watched', he seems to have seen

D

less and less with the outer eye. Mind and landscape become equally still. The passage moves from solitary inquisitiveness, playful in nature, to an exposure even more complete because 'tranquil'. The lines show the influx of a power which is indeed incipient genius, in Wordsworth's terms, to the extent that it is becalmed and imageless. We are reminded of a similar notation of obscure imaginative transience in the repeated phrase in one of the Notebooks associated with Book I: 'The mountains & the fluctuating hills'. The Presences of Nature, Wordsworth said, haunted him in his boyish sports and hieroglyphically 'Impress'd upon all forms the characters/Of danger and desire', making 'the surface of the universal earth . . . Work like a sea' with human hopes and fears. We might take the opening of a later poem, 'Surprised by joy', as a motto for the imagination when, in its commerce with a benevolent universe, it is most active when passive, most creative when exposed to the sublime fluctuations of the earth and its winds and moving waters.

After describing the scene on the naked crag, Wordsworth in the 1805 version of the poem moves directly to describe the human mind as 'fram'd even like the breath/And harmony of music'. Music is often the metaphor for mental unity in *The Prelude*, and in Book II the poet describes with considerable self-identification a solitary musician whose playing composes and animates a shadowy lake. The boys had been playing all afternoon at an inn on the eastern shore of Windermere:

> But ere the fall
> Of night, when in our pinnace we return'd
> Over the dusky Lake, and to the beach
> Of some small Island steer'd our course with one,
> The Minstrel of our troop, and left him there,
> And row'd off gently, while he blew his flute
> Alone, upon the rock; Oh! then the calm
> And dead still water lay upon my mind
> Even with a weight of pleasure, and the sky
> Never before so beautiful, sank down
> Into my heart, and held me like a dream.
>
> (1805, II. 170–80)

It is like those pleasure-barges on Ullswater, fitted by the Duke of Portland with brass cannon mounted on swivels and sent out to rouse the echoes: 'They sailed into the middle of the lake, fired off the guns of their own ego, and waited, patiently yet excitedly, to hear the echoes return to them' (N. Nicholson, *The Lakers: The Adventures of the First Tourists*, 1955). But this passage is subtler too, its image of the isolated minstrel evoking all the high associations of poetic hopes in exact conjunction with a devastating twilit landscape. The relentless, literal monosyllabic force of 'the calm/And dead still water lay upon my mind', and 'the sky . . . sank down/Into my heart' suggest, even here, the responsibility – perhaps the pain – of such complete openness to experience. A 'weight of pleasure' – beauty which can hold someone 'like a dream' – these are conditions fascinating to a child, dangerous for a poet.

Wordsworth comments on the educative value of such scenes for a child:

> Thus daily were my sympathies enlarged,
> And thus the common range of visible things
> Grew dear to me. . . .
>
> (1805, II, 11. 181–3)

For a writer who is trying to show the roots of poetry in common early experiences and in ordinary cognition, 'daily', 'common', and 'visible' will be especially meaningful words. Yet in this instance, as in the whole poem, he perhaps deliberately underestimates the degree to which his double role as experiencer and narrator, listener and minstrel, tends to qualify the 'common range of visible things' by confronting them with an extraordinary, selective, and mature observer.

Wordsworth stitched into Book V a passage on another boyish minstrel, one who actually provokes counter-speech from the landscape. Though these lines were written in Germany in 1798 with himself as protagonist, in the 1800 *Lyrical Ballads* and here in *The Prelude* he consciously masks 'my' with 'his' and 'I' with 'he', pretending a purely narrative interest with third-person distance. Yet the real interest of the passage is not narrative or anecdotal; it lies with the sequence of description:

> There was a Boy: ye knew him well, ye cliffs
> And islands of Winander! – many a time
> At evening, when the earliest stars began
> To move along the edges of the hills,
> Rising or setting, would he stand alone
> Beneath the trees or by the glimmering lake,
> And there, with fingers interwoven, both hands

Pressed closely palm to palm, and to his mouth
Uplifted, he, as through an instrument,
Blew mimic hootings to the silent owls,
That they might answer him; and they would shout
Across the watery vale, and shout again,
Responsive to his call, with quivering peals,
And long halloos and screams, and echoes loud,
Redoubled and redoubled, concourse wild
Of jocund din; and, when a lengthened pause
Of silence came and baffled his best skill,
Then sometimes, in that silence while he hung
Listening, a gentle shock of mild surprise
Has carried far into his heart the voice
Of mountain torrents; or the visible scene
Would enter unawares into his mind,
With all its solemn imagery, its rocks,
Its woods, and that uncertain heaven, received
Into the bosom of the steady lake.

(V, 11. 364–88)

It is in such unfolding strips of language that the meditative mind realizes in sequence landscapes conceived with a purpose. Meditative progress from the descriptive mode to another and deeper kind of thinking by continuing transition is managed with the fewest possible structural articulations, as the passage moves from a hint of ordinary narration ('There was a Boy') to the detailed and ramified explanation of the mystic hootings and the owls' prompt returns.

The owls with their halloos and screams are preparation and transition to the final inevitable lines, their 'jocund din', itself a gift of the scene, contrasting with the ensuing silence of a still deeper apprehension of the universe. Wordsworth in 1815 printed this passage separately, with its coda describing the boy's early death, as the first piece under the heading Poems of the Imagination, and in his Preface he referred to the alertness of the boy's perceptions. The boy, he said, 'is listening, with something of a feverish and restless anxiety, for the recurrence of the riotous sounds which he had previously excited; and, at the moment when the intenseness of his mind is beginning to remit, he is surprised into a perception of the solemn and tranquillizing images which the Poem describes'. The verse achieves this surprise into a perception by working very hard the 'questionings of sense' concealed in human perception of space and time, dimensions which are here virtually demolished in that extraordinary 'lengthened pause' and the paysage intérieur of the final lines. Verb tenses give the impression of simultaneity: the 'shock of mild surprise', the boy's access of being and knowledge, occurs between the past tense of the crucial verb 'hung' (again pivotal at line-end) and the continuous present implied by 'Has carried'. During the intercalary pause of silence 'while he hung/Listening', the boy partakes of the solemnity, steadfast harmony, and greatness of the scene and is himself great.

As in the skating episode, the boy is sportively and even idly quizzing the external world, and the gift of educative perception comes as the kind of recognition (to use one of Wordsworth's favourite terms), religious in nature, which asks that a person change and intensify his living. Again, 'heart' and 'mind' are given spatial images, as in the response to sound over water in the Book II passage quoted above. Though at the confrontation mind and world interpenetrate deeply, Wordsworth preserves their distinction. 'Far into his heart' and 'enter . . . his mind' are expressions which contain a deliberate ambiguity, being at once assertions of astonishing literal impossibility and recognizable metaphors for the burden of consciousness. Such formulations, objective and subjective at the same time, are conceived by Wordsworth as the natural language for childhood consciousness in its exposure to 'the regular action of the world'.

At one point in Book II, Wordsworth speaks of the grandeur of those early times of openness and solitary exposure, wondering 'How shall I trace the history, where seek/The origin' of his 'first creative sensibility'. He says that:

> Oft in those moments such a holy calm
> Would overspread my soul, that bodily eyes
> Were utterly forgotten, and what I saw
> Appeared like something in myself, a dream,
> A prospect in the mind.

(II, 11. 346–50)

The imagination even in childhood knows the forms of experience prefiguratively and all is rehearsed before it happens. On the other hand, adult memory will return to past experience, so that life itself may sometimes seem more mental than actual when the mature poet is 'not used to make/A present joy the matter of my Song'. (1805, I, 11. 55–6). Thus in Wordsworth the question whether knowledge is

43

possible – whether nature in the form of landscape does in fact have an educative function – needs continual answering in the affirmative by fresh encounter with the world, and this continual reformulation is achieved in the account of childhood growth in the early books of the poem.

3

Wordsworth says that he could wish his days 'to be/Bound each to each by natural piety' so that the childhood consciousness could be easily, naturally repossessed. 'Piety' or 'holy calm' applied to childhood experience is to him the fit reverence for a time when boyish sports bring intuitions about the universe, when children may 'sport upon the shore' of the sea of immortality. Yet at the other end of life there is for Wordsworth another category of extremity, composed of all the impassive Solitaries and Wanderers in his poems, men full of age and monotonous experience who are nevertheless touched by a special grace of endurance. These withered yet persisting figures have a kinship in endurance which Wordsworth suggests by submerging their personal identities in the titles of their conditions: the Old Cumberland Beggar, the Discharged Soldier, the Leech Gatherer. They are more profoundly important than Wordsworth's shepherds and dalesmen in peopling the landscape because their personal desolation tends to make of them – without reducing their humanity – an indeterminate thing between man and his environment, walking and testifying fragments of the landscape.

In 'The Old Cumberland Beggar', by indirection suggesting his own response as poet to such wanderers, Wordsworth says that certain lofty meditative minds will create lasting human happiness:

> even such minds
> In childhood, from this solitary Being,
> Or from like wanderer, haply have received . . .
> That first mild touch of sympathy and thought,
> In which they found their kindred with a world
> Where want and sorrow were.

(c.f. 11. 105–16)

Such figures, if they appeared at all in eighteenth-century writing, were ornamental – hermits or banditti who would enhance the atmosphere of a scene. But Wordsworth makes them the focus of value, blessed and blessing because in the lap of nature they convey a single message, that 'man is dear to man' and 'that we have all of us one human heart'. Without contradicting their natural environment, their existence yet has something to teach about human consciousness which is more explicit and monitory than the always indefinite lessons of sheer or unpeopled landscape. The 'first mild touch of sympathy and thought' is more easily brought about, for a mind fascinated by the forms of nature, by the presence of a man who has begun to blend back into the earth and who shares its steadfastness. The Old Cumberland Beggar baffles Wordsworth's sense of time: 'Him from my childhood I have known; and then/He was so old, he seems not older now.' Though they appear beyond change, even the solitaries must go on existing and continue wandering dispossessed and fighting the weather – figures involved in that exposure which is hope, resolution, and independence.

As early as 1797 in 'The Old Cumberland Beggar' Wordsworth is referring to a solitary as emblematic. In a headnote he made it clear that this was a special beggar, of a class soon to be extinct, who would make the stated round of a neighbourhood for provisions. Much of the poem is an explicit discussion of the beggar's moral significance to the community: 'deem not this man useless – Statesmen!' The argument in his defence is from the utility of feeling aroused, the production of generosity in others. Still another argument, less formal but we may imagine closer to Wordsworth's deepest personal concern, is to be found in the particulars of the opening description and the closing plea for independence in exposure:

> In the sun,
> Upon the second step of that small pile,
> Surrounded by those wild unpeopled hills,
> He sat, and ate his food in solitude. . . .

(ll. 12–15)

> He travels on, a solitary Man;
> His age has no companion. On the ground
> His eyes are turned, and, as he moves along,
> They move along the ground; and, evermore,
> Instead of common and habitual sight
> Of fields with rural works, of hill and dale,
> And the blue sky, one little span of earth
> Is all his prospect.

(ll. 44–51)

45

... long as he can wander, let him breathe
The freshness of the valleys; let his blood
Struggle with frosty air and winter snows;
And let the chartered wind that sweeps the heath
Beat his grey locks against his withered face. . . .

(11. 172–6)

And let him, where and when he will, sit down
Beneath the trees, or on a grassy bank
Of highway side, and with the little birds
Share his chance-gathered meal; and, finally,
As in the eye of Nature he has lived,
So in the eye of Nature let him die!

(1. 192-end)

The beggar's helplessness and solitude are touched on at every point, perhaps nowhere more remarkably than in the description of his 'Bow-bent' carriage and the limitation of his vision to 'one little span of earth' where he sees straw, leaves, wheel-marks. The striking metaphysical reversal of the 'prospect' convention (1. 51) is a representative image of dwindled faculties and a relentless stripping-down to essential being. Human, yet blended into the spare society of 'wild unpeopled hills' and 'small mountain birds', the beggar seems almost an emblem of the possibility of vital connection with the natural world when childhood has been left behind. But to Wordsworth, who supplies the loving details of the man's consciousness, such a life is – like a child's – a wordless poem, unique and defying all reduction to mere emblem or utility. Most important, breathing and living in 'that vast solitude to which/The tide of things has borne him', he weathers his exposure and retains human status despite the transience and solitude of life in the eye or very centre of a kindly universe.

The style and phrasing of these descriptions resemble portions of the story of Wordsworth's meeting with the discharged soldier, which was written at the same period (early 1798) and which ends Book IV of *The Prelude*. The encounter with the soldier, however, is entirely descriptive, and the absorbing of normative interest into the particulars of the soldier's attitude, dress and speech – within the larger autobiographical frame with its first-person directness – marks an advance in method. By means of a passage later interpolated, Wordsworth manages to move into the account by apt recollection of his pleasure in wandering alone on public roads; the chance apparition of the soldier becomes a lesson, the substance of which is in his description itself:

> His arms were long, and bare his hands; his mouth
> Shew'd ghastly in the moonlight; from behind
> A milestone propp'd him, and his figure seem'd
> Half-sitting, and half-standing. I could mark
> That he was clad in military garb,
> Though faded, yet entire. He was alone,
> Had no attendant, neither Dog, nor Staff,
> Nor knapsack; in his very dress appear'd
> A desolation, a simplicity
> That seem'd akin to solitude.
>
> (1805, IV, ll. 410–19)

'Faded, yet entire', the military clothing is the outer image of the soldier's mind. 'Nor . . . could I forbear/To question him of what he had endur'd,' says Wordsworth, quizzing all his seasoned wanderers thus, seeking hints of the humanizing exposure of the period of full manhood upon which he is entering. The soldier's answer is delivered with 'a strange half-absence' as of a man 'Remembering the importance of his theme/But feeling it no longer'. This is perhaps the ideal state of the poet who recollects in tranquillity the distress of an earlier passion; but perhaps too it is a separation of the feeling from the relevance of a story, an avoidance of the risk of feeling – whether from slowly hardened insensibility or from deliberate personal retreat.

Like the 'Old Man Travelling' (written 1797), the great Solitaries move with thought, not pain, and are 'insensibly subdued/To settled quiet'. They have earned the peace which comes only after attrition of experience, but in the process they have become grotesques with a 'ghastly mildness' who are represented as being unable, verbally at least, to divulge their secrets. Even language has lost its power of life: like the 'speaking crags' and vocal hills elsewhere in Wordsworth, these men give their humanizing histories ventriloquially, through the medium of description and external paraphrase. They give more pointed animation to a scene than landscape; but not much more. Their special interest in any study of Wordsworthian landscape will lie in the way a history of the solitaries from 'The Old Cumberland Beggar' (1797) to the Wanderer and Solitary of *The Excursion* (1814), reveals a gradually more explicit change in the poet's views on personal exposure and openness to experience. After 1798–9 we see him beginning to undertake 'exposure' as a programme of personal development – with respect now to human suffering or sorrow instead of the action of the world and its surrogate landscapes. The 'first mild touch of sympathy and thought' hinted in 'The Old Cumberland Beggar' has become a heavy hand in *The Excursion*.

The process is particularly clear in 'Resolution and Independence' (1802), which comes between early (1798–9) and later (1804–5) portions of *The Prelude*. With its explicit jostling of the poet's self-consciousness and the solutions of the great Solitaries, the poem allies itself with the tone and concerns of the later *Prelude*, openly announcing what is only implicit in the profound despair recorded in the two books (XI and XII in the version of 1805) titled 'Imagination and Taste, how Impaired and Restored'; namely, the axiom that 'We Poets in our youth begin in gladness;/But thereof come in the end despondency and madness'. In one of the first decisions which shows him thinking in terms of deliberate emblem, Wordsworth changes the title of the poem from 'The Leech Gatherer' to 'Resolution and Independence'. The method of the poem is to enforce progressive transition. An opening landscape, where the speaker is as usual a 'Traveller', gives way by degrees to an encounter with the old leech gatherer wherein the poet eagerly repeats his question 'How is it that you live, and what is it you do?' The animated and perfectly detailed landscape, which sets the action in a dense natural setting, fills but does not clutter Wordsworth's rime-royal stanzas:

> All things that love the sun are out of doors;
> The sky rejoices in the morning's birth;
> The grass is bright with rain-drops; – on the moors
> The hare is running races in her mirth;
> And with her feet she from the plashy earth
> Raises a mist; that, glittering in the sun,
> Runs with her all the way, wherever she doth run.
>
> (stanza II)

'The image of the hare I . . . observed on the ridge of the [Barton] fell' is his comment in the circumstantial Fenwick note to the poem. Here as elsewhere Wordsworth likes to juxtapose etched, accurate observation like that of the mist which 'Runs . . . all the way' with the hare, with generalization and obvious pathetic fallacy ('The sky rejoices').

The speaker identifies his mood with the joy of this scene, but suddenly he reverts from delight to dejection, from bodily sensing to 'blind thoughts', feeling now his difference from the things and creatures he perceives. Mind and world become separable, even rival, dispensations. And the rest of the poem, despite token gestures at landscape, is an exploration of the gap between mind and world as it affects the maturing poet, and the questionings are moral and psychological. The figure in the scene succeeds the landscape as the focus of interest. The splendidly detailed landscape which opens the poem has thus in fact been employed as the introduction to a movement of the mind towards possible avenues of honourable affirmation and personal security; by implication, we see that these will be the poet's new grounds for writing. Having thus performed its work the landscape is left behind. Or, more precisely and still more revealing, it is in a few descriptive touches changed in tone and function to a 'weary moor', the apt image of the leech gatherer's condition.

The opening landscape works by incremental detail and catalogue, rather like the short poem 'Written in March' (1802), which dates only two months earlier in composition. There is the same tranced listing of things heard and seen, all in the same joyous key. The effect is perfect in a charming way:

> The Cock is crowing,
> The stream is flowing,
> The small birds twitter,
> The lake doth glitter,
> The green field sleeps in the sun;
> The oldest and youngest
> Are at work with the strongest;
> The cattle are grazing,
> Their heads never raising;
> There are forty feeding like one!

But 'Resolution and Independence' repudiates this kind of perception as inadequate, undercutting statements like 'Even such a happy Child of earth am I' by the more serious cataloguing of 'Solitude, pain of heart, distress, and poverty' (stanza V). The leech gatherer is in his person the final impeachment of spontaneous joy, and of dejection as well, for the old man is past fluctuations of consciousness: 'as a huge stone', he is somehow at one with the bleak earth: 'Motionless as a cloud' yet a wanderer exposed to 'Employment hazardous and wearisome'. Like the other Solitaries his presence seems 'A leading from above, a something given'. Though ravaged by age, he has 'yet-vivid eyes' and 'a stately speech' and his endurance seems an admonishment to the perplexed, unstable poet.

Wordsworth avoids elaborate detail in description of the man's appearance for the same reason he avoids direct speech. Like a 'composed' landscape the 'whole body' of the leech gatherer is one and harmonious, a pure instance of the life of imagination lived not in childhood but in conscious maturity. His presence takes account of the reduction of capacities and hopes which must come with maturity: this is the reason for the bleak setting of 'A pool bare to the eye of heaven', the symbolic dwindling of the leeches, the extremity of the old man's life and physique. The man transcends circumstance by the prior and continuing exertion of integrity, and how this can be remains unexamined: 'Whether it were by peculiar grace/ A leading from above, a something given/Yet it befell . . .' (stanza VIII). Like the growing child he does not need to speak – he is. 'What is brought forward?' Wordsworth comments on the poem in a letter: '"A lonely place, a pond" "by which an old man *was*, far from all house or home" – not stood, not sat, but "was" – the figure presented in the most naked simplicity possible.' But the problem of the necessity of language is beginning to be posed here with something like desperation. When the observer is not the child confronted with a teaching landscape, but a perplexed adult who is 'longing to be comforted', a poet confronted with an admonishing human figure, the response can hardly be divorced from language and remain adequate. Thus it prefigures the uncertainty of the poems to come that 'Resolution and Independence' should in its final two stanzas present two different endings:

> In my mind's eye I seemed to see him pace
> About the weary moors continually,
> Wandering about alone and silently.
>
> (stanza XIX)

> 'God', said I, 'be my help and stay secure;
> I'll think of the Leech-gatherer on the lonely moor!'
>
> (stanza XX)

The true ending is the magnificent image of extremity and exposure, the actual ending is a flat concession to conventional morality.

A final image of solitary exposure may be added, one which brings together much of what has been said of Wordsworth's gradual withdrawal from a concern with innocence and landscape. 'Elegiac

Stanzas, Suggested by a Picture of Peele Castle, in a Storm, Painted by Sir George Beaumont' uses the metaphor of Beaumont's picture to organize honest ironies about the false or picturesque, and the true response to a scene. The picture is the nominal centre of a conflict between a seascape of imagined innocence which radiated 'the light that never was on sea or land,/The consecration and the poet's dream' and an image of experience which shows 'the sea in anger' with 'the dismal shore'. But the real organizing centre, hidden outside the poem, is the death of Wordsworth's brother John, who went down with the ship which was his first command. Wordsworth first received news of the drowning in February 1805, and wrote the poem later in the year with the conviction that 'A power is gone which nothing can restore;/A deep distress hath humanised my soul'. It is the word 'humanised' which indicates the direction of the change of subject which will also be a change of style; a new faith is needed which can naturalize such distress.

Wordsworth describes Beaumont's picture by praising the moral as well as visual composition of the details. It is 'a passionate Work' whose 'spirit' is 'well chosen' because every part – the sea with its heaving boat, the sky, 'this pageantry of fear' – bespeak a murderous nature. But Peele Castle itself as the leading subject is described in a dense quatrain as presenting the stoic defensive alternative; the castle becomes one of the noblest of the unspeaking solitaries:

> And this huge Castle, standing here sublime,
> I love to see the look with which it braves,
> Cased in the unfeeling armour of old time,
> The lightning, the fierce wind, and trampling waves.

Exposure and seclusion are combined in the heroic image of consciousness as a fortress. Wordsworth draws on writers like Burke and Alison for his notion that enduring objects are properly sublime, but he presses further than they do, in his belief that sublimity can be an attribute of the suffering human mind when it braves its appropriate terrors with only the armour of accumulated experience. In 'Tintern Abbey' he did not mention the abbey itself; his turn to the architecture of a scene, like his turn to the Solitaries, is a movement away from such metaphors of internal and external mutuality as the breeze and the river, and evidence that the 'power' which is irrecoverably gone is an unsuspecting love of landscape for its own sake.

4

In *The Prelude*, Wordsworth shows himself not unaware of the issues
involved in a withdrawal from landscape, but it is difficult to speak
more positively about the extent of his recognitions. A poem about
the genesis and composition of poetry, when it is tied to the premise
of personal growth, can hardly evade the complexities and still demand assent to the end. But already, in 'Tintern Abbey', he spoke with
candour of childhood:

> That time is past,
> And all its aching joys are now no more,
> And all its dizzy raptures. Not for this
> Faint I, nor mourn nor murmur; other gifts
> Have followed; for such loss, I would believe,
> Abundant recompense.

'I would believe' may stand as the summary of 'Tintern Abbey' and
The Prelude taken as a whole; the meditative poems are assertions of
belief, always to some extent written in order to convince, quiet, or
crush his unbelief. He was not the kind of man to ask his unbelief to
help his belief; sympathetic imagination never, in his case, reached
the point of Keatsian negative capability. Again, the retrospective
method, where the poem attempts to bend back towards previous
states of mind, has always the possible result of shortchanging the
present, subordinating it in grandeur and promise to the past. This
may well have been the impasse which delayed him several years in
finding a satisfactory context for the stunning episodes which make
up the first books of *The Prelude*.

The long poem begins with an unconventional search for a subject, in the midst of personal freedom and a congenial breezy landscape; but as it gathers momentum, bringing the narrative closer to
the present day, fewer risks are taken and the story is manipulated
to an ending 'All gratulant, if rightly understood' (XIV, 1. 388), with
a theory of the mind as antagonistic to sensation. Wordsworth describes the years spent at Cambridge as benign enough: he was
'detached/Internally from academic cares' (1805, VI, 11. 29–30).
But with Book VII the spectacle of London looms as unmanageable, a
'press/Of self-destroying, transitory things' (1805, VII, 11. 738–9)

where in the 'overflowing streets' he would say to himself 'the face of every one/That passes by me is a mystery' (1805, VII, 11. 596–7). The three books on France, an excursion into humanitarian politics, completely relevant to his narrative of poetic growth, set out to show how freedom as a national and personal ideal becomes instead a threat. Finally the healing retreat to Dorothy and Grasmere, with the adoption of a programme of repossessing 'spots of time' as a conscious poetic method, results in the conclusion, not latent or implied in Books I and II, that 'the mind of man becomes/A thousand times more beautiful than the earth/On which he dwells' (1805, XIII, 446–8).

Though schematic and perhaps unjust, this summary of The Prelude serves to call attention to a change, amounting to a reversal, in Wordsworth's notions of exposure to the workings of the world. We may put it briefly by contending that, while early in his writing life 'the world' found its locus in educative rugged landscapes of the Lake District and the Alps, later on and increasingly 'the world' came to mean society, institutions, the locus of human bereavement and suffering. The great poems of 1798–1807 were written as he felt his way towards man: 'Farewell, farewell, the heart that lives alone,/ Housed in a dream, at distance from the Kind!' ('Elegiac Stanzas'). Since he was never entirely able to jettison the landscape premises of 1798, his landscape poems are humanitarian and his avowedly philosophical poems, The Prelude and The Excursion, keep returning to landscape as value.

Two contrasting mountain descriptions in The Prelude – the Simplon Pass descent (Book VI) and the Snowdon Climb (Book XIV in the 1850 version) – best illustrate the effects on the poetry of a change in Wordsworth's mode of regard. The consummation and triumph of the baptized imagination in the last book of the poem is no mere discursive declaration but a fully detailed 'excursion' up the highest mountain in England and Wales. After a plodding climb up Snowdon at night 'with forehead bent/Earthward', a flash from the uncovered moon at an immense height reveals, at Wordsworth's feet, 'a silent sea of hoary mist':

> A hundred hills their dusky backs upheaved
> All over this still ocean; and beyond,
> Far, far beyond, the solid vapours stretched,
> In headlands, tongues, and promontory shapes,
> Into the main Atlantic, that appeared

> To dwindle, and give up his majesty,
> Usurped upon far as the sight could reach.
>
> (XIV, 11. 43–49)

The moon seems to compose the scene; yet, as David Ferry has argued, this 'beautiful and predictable symbol of the powers of the imagination or of that divine Power which is the source of all imaginations, controlling and ordering the visible world', has in fact a massive earthly antagonist in the roar of moving waters (*The Limits of Mortality*, 1959). Beneath the gazing moon the submissive ocean lay 'all meek and silent save that' – and it is a concession made more overwhelming in the 1850 wording:

> save that through a rift –
> Not distant from the shore whereon we stood,
> A fixed, abysmal, gloomy, breathing-place –
> Mounted the roar of waters, torrents, streams
> Innumerable, roaring with one voice!
> Heard over earth and sea, and, in that hour,
> For so it seemed, felt by the starry heavens.
>
> (11. 56–62)

Wordsworth asserts a composition of appearance, but the antinomies of the scene remain unmanageable; it is earth against sky, ear against eye. Imagination finds its 'image' – indeed the 1850 text changes this to 'type' and 'emblem' – in the 'abysmal, gloomy', deafening realm where no human could exist.

So the vision Wordsworth saved for a flourish at the end, even supplying it with a long commentary to squeeze significance from phenomena observed and heard, becomes an allegory of inhuman exposure. Finally the natural scene is not used but obliterated. In this last Book, Wordsworth does not abandon the landscape convention of the excursion or tour, but uses it for his changed purposes. Often in later poems he draws on the same landscapes and locales as earlier poems, even the same images of exposure and peril, though his 'humanised' intention leads him to dwell on different details and to read his landscapes as systematic emblems. His title *The Excursion* is thus incorrect; as he seems himself to have in part suspected, *The Recluse* is the fit label for poems, written after 1805, which possess an unconsciously qualified conviction of the love of man.

It is in this light that his central image of exposure, the descent from the Simplon Pass through the Gondo Gorge, may seem a truer report on an excursion into the world; and this despite its similar concern for the aspirations of the human mind towards the infinite, despite even its refusal to render descriptive details as matter of fact. Wordsworth had already rehearsed his alpine journey by the time he took it up in The Prelude as contributing to his poetic growth: in a letter of picturesque piety and awe to Dorothy, written on the spot in Switzerland (1790), and in 'Descriptive Sketches' (1793) where he put snapshots of alpine scenery into heroic couplets. Though there are few hints of the passage on the descent in these early descriptions, their presence means he had already twice composed the context and external frame of the journey. At the time, in 1790 and 1793, the scene had for him no unity of appearance. The ecstasy following on the recognition 'That we had crossed the Alps', the profound gloom during the slow descent of the gorge, are modifications of the meditative intelligence which would have been out of key with the tenor and style of 'Descriptive Sketches'. Years of brooding and a return to the key of melancholy desolation which the 'Sketches' had briefly noted (line 251), encouraged his 'original gift of spreading the tone, the *atmosphere*, and with it the depth and height of the ideal world around forms, incidents, and situations', to borrow Coleridge's words on a far inferior poem.

In fact, then, it is lapse of time and subsequent intentional re-encounter in the act of writing which composes the scene:

> The dull and heavy slackening that ensued
> Upon those tidings by the Peasant given
> Was soon dislodg'd; downwards we hurried fast,
> And enter'd with the road which we had miss'd
> Into a narrow chasm; the brook and road
> Were fellow-travellers in this gloomy Pass,
> And with them did we journey several hours
> At a slow step. The immeasurable height
> Of woods decaying, never to be decay'd,
> The stationary blasts of water-falls,
> And every where along the hollow rent
> Winds thwarting winds, bewilder'd and forlorn,
> The torrents shooting from the clear blue sky,
> The rocks that mutter'd close upon our ears,
> Black drizzling crags that spake by the way-side
> As if a voice were in them, the sick sight

And giddy prospect of the raving stream,
The unfetter'd clouds, and region of the Heavens,
Tumult and peace, the darkness and the light
Were all like workings of one mind, the features
Of the same face, blossoms upon one tree,
Characters of the great Apocalypse,
The types and symbols of Eternity,
Of first and last, and midst, and without end.

(1805, VI, ll. 549–72)

The description differs from the Snowdon ascent primarily in its success in doing what it claims, in composing violent antinomies of perception. This is one of those moments when there is no question that it is the remembering mind and not some surrogate of mind in the scene – such as moon and heavenly vault as commanding emblems of order in the Snowdon scene – which imposes the order, physiognomy, and restrained personification. Yet the actual scene persists as the occasion for the reminiscence and the fund of images drawn upon for its description.

A plain topographical narrative voice continues until, at mid-line, a more dignified Orphic voice takes over with a long column of meditative observation. In effect this ellipse of thought at line 556 marks the moment of separation, the time when the speaker forgets he has 'bodily eyes' and what he sees appears 'like something in myself, a dream,/A prospect in the mind' (as Wordsworth says in 1805, II, ll. 369–71). Yet it is still, for the moment, but a 'giddy prospect', a 'sick sight' – uncomposed and all but deranged in its intensity. Perhaps the unity that underlies these disjunctions of appearance is to be sought first not in analysis of presented detail, but in the full appreciation of such purely technical mastery as the elimination of that true metaphor, or conceit, which to Wordsworth is merely a mode of the fancy; the sophisticated qualifications 'as if' and 'like'; and the use of unobtrusive but crucial affirmative words: 'all', 'one', 'same'. The long unbroken sentence beginning 'The immeasurable height' catalogues paradoxes of time and space, optical illusion, pathetic fallacy, allowing utmost variation in the pausing with a large number of impetuous run-on lines. But finally it enforces order, moving to assertions of harmony in the bounded one-line units and a conclusive last line which confirms one's sense that the reconciliation of opposites is the method of the passage. The Snowdon vision affirms a unity in the scene which it does not find, but needs; but the

Simplon descent, presenting the whole scene in terms of visible con-
flicts, finds its reconciliation in the invisible – in the mind of the
poet and the mind of God.

5

By reference, then, to the actual details of the scenes as Wordsworth
describes them, it is possible to judge one abstract rhetoric more
fully earned and realized than another. No writer before Wordsworth
urges to such a degree that poetry be verified by reference to possible
ordinary perceptions. The descriptive is the base and the rhetoric, let
us say, of apocalypse (in VI, 11. 568–72), is finally more expressive
of formative experience than the rhetoric of emblem. This is because
the Simplon rhetoric sorts almost perfectly with the descriptive
medium which it flowers from and then replaces within the single
sentence. The poetry modulates from description to meditation:
there is no disjunction when Wordsworth moves to the educative
aspects of the images of exposure, and in this respect the passage
merely condenses and exemplifies the import of those passages on
'spots of time' and solitary humans which recur so often in his
poetry.

In the *Guide to the Lakes* (1810) Wordsworth opens his description
of the scenery of the Lakes with a View of the Country as formed by
Nature. He then passes, in his second section, to the Aspect of the
Country, as affected by its Inhabitants, and this he begins by asking
the reader to envisage what the landscape, finished by the great im-
personal forces of nature and awaiting its first human inhabitants,
looked like in its primeval freshness. Characteristically the prose,
having fulfilled its descriptive function, shades off into the larger concerns of the poetry. As from a prospect elevated in time and space,
the reader 'looks down upon this scene':

> He will form to himself an image of the tides visiting and
> revisiting the friths, the main sea dashing against the
> bolder shore, the rivers pursuing their course to be lost in
> the mighty mass of waters. He may see or hear in fancy
> the winds sweeping over the lakes, or piping with a loud
> voice among the mountain peaks; and, lastly, may think

57

of the primaeval woods shedding and renewing their leaves with no human eye to notice or human heart to welcome the change.

Here, as in the Simplon passage, Wordsworth holds in poise a sense both of the identity and divorce of inner and outer nature, and while he imagines the absence of imagination he consciously demonstrates that faculty at its highest pitch.

3
Peopling the landscape

I

A study of landscape needs to touch only lightly on the larger question of Wordsworth's concept of nature. Here I need merely observe that with Rousseau, Blake, and Wordsworth, nature – previously the order of things and the imitator of man – becomes a critique of men and institutions. Between 1720–1810 the march of intellect leads through a complete swing of interest towards the wild, sublime natural forms of mountain and ocean whose obscurity, greatness, and infinity could be described as beyond human conception. Recurring Romantic epithets such as 'the trackless ocean' express economically the alien sense of outer nature, its mystery and resistance to formulation. Aesthetic theory, with its belief in the composition of a measured scene out of the welter of appearance, tacitly acknowledges this: as the theorist of the Picturesque, William Gilpin, had it, 'the scale of nature . . . so different from your scale'. The subjective reading of perception fostered by Rousseau, Kant, Alison, and others, was at the same time an appeal to the otherness of the objects of perception.

It is true of course that older expectations did not disappear entirely: in 1808 a critic of Richard Wilson objected to his later Welsh landscapes, paintings unmediated by classical or picturesque arrangements: 'Remove the ruined temples, palaces, and columns, you exhibit a naked nature, which, however wild and grand, will have lost its power over the heart.' Yet this naked nature was precisely the thing desired by the painters and poets of the new generation. The sublime landscape, the real language of men, the noble savage, were ideas at once of escape and of critique, normative and persuasive in their literary use, and as conventional and mythological in their way as the beliefs of the old dispensation they were supplanting.

Eighteenth-century landscapists often neglected Keats's wholesome qualification that 'scenery is fine – but Human Nature is finer'. But Wordsworth, despite his profoundest conviction that a sublime and naked nature is finer, came increasingly to assert the pre-eminence of the figure in the scene. The bridge from scenery to society, from a largely aesthetic to an ethical appreciation of the

59

natural world was to be his notion of the educative value of landscape. Somehow, though, Wordsworth could never make these arguments quite convincing; wherever expressed, they are attended by a
prescriptive moral rhetoric and by a darkening view of nature. Of
course, what is of interest is not so much the second-order speculative
verse which contains the argument, as the massive stubbornness of
the endeavour to humanize nature and his art.

From about the time of Wordsworth's birth, landscape in painting and poetry found the human figure difficult to integrate in scenes
increasingly wild and sublime. This limitation, central to the question of the adequacy of the landscape genre to the portrayal of a full
image of man, is perhaps most succinctly expressed in the literature
of painting. Gilpin, for instance, subordinates character to environment on principle:

> Moral, and picturesque ideas do not always coincide. . . .
> In a moral view, the industrious mechanic is a more
> pleasing object, than the loitering peasant. But in a pic-
> turesque light, it is otherwise. The arts of industry are
> rejected; and even idleness, if I may so speak, adds
> dignity to character.

Richard Wilson, like Gilpin, regarded the human figure not as essential or ennobling, but as a technical device: he looked on men, it was
said, 'as they composed harmoniously':

> One day, looking on the fine scene from Richmond
> Terrace, and wishing to point out a spot of particular
> beauty to a friend . . ., 'There,' said he, holding out his
> finger, 'see near those houses, – there, where the figures
> are.'

Wordsworth himself preferred the generalization of human figures
when the primary interest of a painting was descriptive:

> Wordsworth said He thought Historical subjects shd.
> never be introduced into Landscape, but where the Land-
> scape was to be subservient to them. – Where the Land-
> scape was intended principally to impress the mind,
> figures, other than such as are general . . . are injurious to
> the effect which the Landscape shd. produce as a scene
> founded on the observation of nature.

The axiom is recorded in the *Diary* of Joseph Farington (28 April

1807); even in casual conversation Wordsworth returns to the theme which dominates his poems, that of the disjunction, the disproportion, between figure and scene.

In the poetry, Wordsworth's place-affection and love of seclusion are evidently attempts to correct this disproportion. As the first piece in his Poetical Works, he selects a poem invoking his 'Dear native regions' in the counties of Cumberland and Westmorland – a poem which praises the 'local sympathy' of a writer's 'backward view' at the landscapes of his youth. Nearly all his writing was to unfold the same retrospective panorama, and all we know about Wordsworth's life after 1805 confirms his later poetry's yearning for the security of homely sympathy, for meditative seclusion amounting to isolation. Similarly, *The Prelude* promises to show how the pleasures of imagination, at first marvellously individual and self-centred, grow into mature sympathy with man. 'Love of Nature Leading to Love of Man' was a contention, as John Jones says, which Wordsworth 'failed many times to prove . . . but found a kind of poetic salvation in his striving' (*The Egotistical Sublime*, 1954). While deepening his local sympathies, the lure of the proposed philosophical poem, *The Recluse*, where according to Coleridge he was to 'assume the situation of a man in mental repose, one whose principles were made up, and so prepared to deliver upon authority a system of philosophy', seems to have obscured the possibility that sooner or later an unearned repose and seclusion will withdraw the sustaining imagery of the real which a poetry of experience needs for survival.

In depending upon a spatial mapping of the self in a known landscape, Wordsworth is broadly representative of nineteenth-century English writers. From *Lyrical Ballads* to Hardy's *Wessex Poems*, poems and novels are rich in travellers, wanderers on public roads or high seas, whose motions would appear to represent the very evolving unity of experience. Yet, often within the confines of the same poem or novel, such pilgrims have their dialectical counterparts in citizens who believe that place is the only reality and the true fulfilment. Wordsworth himself in *The Prelude* interweaves images of personal exposure – the bird- and boat-stealing episodes, the descent of the Simplon Pass – with images of meditative seclusion in the nooks, valleys, and cottages of the Lake District. The all but obsessive Wordsworthian images of seclusion may be taken as one clue to why landscape, though it was, as Kenneth Clark has observed, the 'chief artistic creation' and 'dominant art' of the century, was so often found vulnerable to the charge of being art for its own sake. In painting and poetry, the question was of humanizing or peopling the landscape by a mode of regard which at best, in Geoffrey Hartman's words, 'will not make a distinction of genre between the human subject and the subject from nature'. Such vision, we may assume, would mean the salutary alternation of exposure and seclusion, a way of bringing meditative habits to bear on events of personal and communal importance, and of forming values by opening the mature self to the flux of experience. Precisely here the example of Wordsworth is most representative, for landscape is joy, escape, and social criticism at different times as he finds his way out of self-preoccupation and eventually far from landscape in itself. The poems of this transition are his finest: in them we watch him trying with larger and larger capaciousness to find what it means to be humanized by time and suffering. As Wordworth comes to explore many of the side-issues of what it means to be a responsibly mature moral artist, he inevitably and rightly – but often with the desolation which obtains when one tampers with an early love – begins to question the adequacy of landscape.

In their genesis and repossession those 'spots of time' which for Wordsworth have a 'renovating virtue' are at once spatial and temporal. Throughout The Prelude he describes the circumstantial location of these vivid episodes, and in the Prospectus to the 1814 Excursion he calls the mind of man 'My haunt, and the main region of my song'. Again, Book I of The Prelude is not unique when in the opening lines it implies that a certain spot or nook – a Vale or Hermitage (1. 115) far from the prisoning city – is required to preside over and indeed evoke the poem. Before he can write, Wordsworth needs a place to write: this is the import of 'Home at Grasmere' (1800), the first and only part of The Recluse proper which he completed, a poem which begins like The Prelude with the narrator's 'unfettered liberty' and his thoughts at a fine elevated prospect:

> The Station whence he look'd was soft and green,
> Not giddy yet aerial, with a depth
> Of vale below, a height of hills above.
> For rest of body, perfect was the Spot,
> All that luxurious nature could desire,
> But stirring to the spirit; who could gaze
> And not feel motions there?
>
> (PW, vol. V, Appendix A, 11. 19–25)

Even as a boy, Wordsworth says, he had decided here 'Must be his

Home, this Valley be his World', and when as a man he returns to
'the calmest, fairest spot of earth' it is 'On Nature's invitation . . .
By Reason sanctioned'. To him, quite literally, the setting is his
emotion, a container whose meditative seclusion he believes he will
partake. For a poet who defines unity of being as an acute sense of
place, 'spot' becomes a metaphysical concept.

'Embrace me, then, ye Hills, and close me in' is Wordsworth's
invocation in 'Home at Grasmere'. The love of enclosure in a
domestic landscape, a deep pastoral valley with its cluster of church
and cottages, leads from local to universal. Grasmere, whose 'lofty
barriers break the force/Of winds', is the outer sign of an internal
grace, 'A Power and protection for the mind' (1. 377) which gives

>   the sense
> Of majesty, and beauty, and repose,
> A blended holiness of earth and sky,
> Something that makes this individual Spot,
> This small Abiding-place of many Men,
> A termination, and a last retreat,
> A Centre, come from wheresoe'er you will,
> A Whole without dependence or defect,
> Made for itself; and happy in itself,
> Perfect Contentment, Unity entire.
>
>   (11. 142–51)

There is a density and significance of life in the human experience
and outer objects of Grasmere Vale which makes it peculiarly apt for
the uses of art:

> Look where we will, some human heart has been
> Before us with its offering. . . .
> Joy spreads, and sorrow spreads; and this whole Vale,
> Home of untutored Shepherds as it is,
> Swarms with sensation, as with gleams of sunshine,
> Shadows or breezes, scents or sounds.
>
>   (1. 440 f.)

We may compare with this Hardy's Little Hintock as it is described in
The Woodlanders:

> It was one of those sequestered spots outside the gates of
> the world where may usually be found more meditation
> than action, and more listlessness than meditation; where
> reasoning proceeds on narrow premises, and results in

inferences wildly imaginative; yet where, from time to time, dramas of a grandeur and unity truly Sophoclean are enacted in the real, by virtue of the concentrated passions and closely-knit inter-dependence of the lives therein.

Hardy permits intellectuals and city-bred intruders into this seclusion and records how the encounter speeds the decline of agriculture and folk-tradition. But Wordsworth tends far more to circumscribe all evil in the city, and is less than candid when, lapsing into abstraction, he claims

> that Labour here preserves
> His rosy face, a Servant only here
> Of the fire-side, or of the open field,
> A Freeman, therefore, sound and unimpaired. . . .
>
> (11. 359–62)

Despite such lapses much of the best rural and agrarian writing in the century – in George Eliot, William Barnes, Richard Jefferies, Hardy – has its debt to Wordsworth's insistence that place may be at once local and universal, whole even in its partiality; that the essential England and real language of men are to be found outside London.

After a summary of poetic strengths, Wordsworth ends 'Home at Grasmere' with the lines 'On Man on Nature and on Human Life' which he later transplanted as the Prospectus to the 1814 edition of *The Excursion*. For the Wordsworth, the search for a place, equivalent to a survey of poetic prowess, becomes a preparation for the humanized imaginative sympathy of the mature man. This is why he wrote, in the same year as 'Home at Grasmere',* a number of *Poems on the Naming of Places*, where in a seriously local poetry he names familiar Grasmere places by their associations with educative guilt or joy. In his Poetical Works, he placed the group immediately after *Poems Founded on the Affections*, intending these poems, he said, 'as a transition to those relating to human life'. In the fourth poem Wordsworth describes a saunter along the eastern shore of Grasmere with his sister Dorothy and Coleridge: they are surprised to find that a man, seen at first 'through a veil of glittering haze' and believed improvident and reckless in harvest season, is in fact gaunt with sickness and fishing 'to gain/A pittance from the dead unfeeling lake'. Their 'happy idleness' is changed to 'self-reproach', and they give the memorial name

* The fifth of these seven poems was written in 1799, the last in 1845. All of the others were conceived and largely completed in 1800.

POINT-RASH-JUDGEMENT to the place of their humanizing admonishment. The other places are named to accord with the qualities and habits of people in Wordsworth's immediate circle: for example Dorothy's name is given to a springtime glen, and 'a cloistral place/Of refuge' in the fir-grove is named for John, whom Wordsworth calls 'A *silent* Poet' because his brother too loves to pace within a solitary covert of the grove. Wordsworth feels these names, which attach affections to rural objects making them worthy memorials, should be apposite, heartfelt, ethical, and above all – however idiosyncratic or local – they must be the results of true perception.

This group of poems proposes naming as the essential poetic act. But the poems perform the act hesitantly, as if Wordsworth refuses to suppress a name like POINT-RASH-JUDGMENT, even though he realizes how personal and arbitrary it must remain. The poems contain a suspicion, at least, that no word touches the heart of things; a suspicion that, as Richard Wilbur says, 'however personally we may take the landscape, however much sympathy and meaning we may discover in it', perhaps 'our words are not anchored in objects at all – that the word *tree* does not harpoon and capture the tree, but merely flies feintingly towards it, and like a boomerang, returns to the hand' ('Poetry and the Landscape', in *The New Landscape*, ed. G. Keypes, 1956). Wordsworth undermines from within his faith in the naming power and in place-affection, complicating his relation to the scenes which are the sources of his art. But neither in these poems nor later on is he fully conscious of the process: never so conscious, for example, as Hardy, whose overwhelming sense of otherness and distance is the withering of Wordsworth's more generous faith. Hardy's blunt ironies most often show how pleasant landscapes and handsome buildings are contradicted by despairing human occupants; but Wordsworth at the beginning of the century can usually convince himself that words touch the heart of things and that seclusion will lead to imaginative transport.

2

The importance of place as a literary motive is most often elegiac and personal; and the image of man to be found in the literature of place and of place revisited is inevitably non-heroic. It seems the very centre of the landscape method that, finally, imagination applied to certain loved details is infinitely more meaningful than imagination applied comprehensively to the world. It is a mode which in the end cannot avoid coping with the world of commonplace perception. Wordsworth tests the limits of his landscape assumptions when he tries to show that there is a non-tragic form of heroism in sheer suffering, in states rather than in active sequences of feeling. This is the reason for the growing importance of the Solitaries in his poetry, unheroic heroes who have been described as virtually at one with their settings. Indeed, as early as *The Borderers* (begun 1795), Wordsworth had made a distinction which cleared his path towards a new kind of poem:

> Action is transitory – a step, a blow,
> The motion of a muscle – this way or that –
> 'Tis done; and in the after-vacancy
> We wonder at ourselves like men betrayed;
> Suffering is permanent, obscure and dark,
> And shares the nature of infinity.

He took these lines from the play for his headnote to 'The White Doe of Rylstone' (1807), a poem which so subordinates its 'fine-spun and inobtrusive' action to the deeper activity of endurance that he could call it 'in conception, the highest work' he had produced. The central character, Emily Norton, last member of a Catholic family devastated in the Rising of the North against the religious oppression of Elizabeth, is according to Wordsworth 'intended to be honoured and loved for what she *endures*, and the manner in which she endures it, accomplishing a conquest over her sorrows (which is the true subject of the poem)'. Wordsworth's use of the verb 'endures' and the noun 'conquest' imply that such suffering is far from passive: that it is in fact what he would term an 'ascent', a more 'permanent' and profound form of being than can be expressed in transitory narrative.

The picture of 'the babe/Nursed in his Mother's arms' in Book II of *The Prelude*, Wordsworth's central image of seclusion, must be understood by a similar reading of the notion of Being. For if his statement is not taken as a boldly figurative ontological statement it will seem almost grotesque as a narrative account of infancy:

Blest the infant Babe,
(For with my best conjecture I would trace
Our Being's earthly progress,) blest the Babe,
Nursed in his Mother's arms, who sinks to sleep
Rocked on his Mother's breast; who with his soul
Drinks in the feelings of his Mother's eye!
For him, in one dear Presence, there exists
A virtue which irradiates and exalts
Objects through widest intercourse of sense.
No outcast he, bewildered and depressed:
Along his infant veins are interfused
The gravitation and the filial bond
Of nature that connect him with the world.

(11. 232–44)

The infant is the image of flawless seclusion, his perception perfectly at one with its objects. 'Emphatically such a Being lives . . . An inmate of this active universe', but, Wordsworth says, this 'first/Poetic spirit of our human life' is in most men 'By uniform control of after years . . . abated or suppressed'. The poetic spirit persists 'through every change of growth and of decay/Pre-eminent till death' only 'in some': certainly it persists in Emily Norton of 'The White Doe', who despite her achieved maturity ascends towards this inner seclusion, made child-like by suffering.

Particularly in Wordsworth's images of nooks and glades, domiciles, ruins, and valleys – features of the scene which represent the desire for seclusion – there is often a curious insensitivity to the issues his landscapes raise. It is very much a question of having an experience and missing the meaning, the full meaning. For instance, three of the seven *Poems on the Naming of Places* deal with the finding of secret nooks, and one of these describes a springtime ramble 'Alive to all things and forgetting all':

At length I to a sudden turning came
In this continuous glen, where down a rock
The Stream, so ardent in its course before,
Sent forth such sallies of glad sound, that all
Which I till then had heard, appeared the voice
Of common pleasure: beast and bird, the lamb,
The shepherd's dog, the linnet and the thrush,
Vied with this waterfall, and made a song,
Which, while I listened, seemed like the wild growth

> Or like some natural produce of the air,
> That could not cease to be.
> ('It was an April morning', 11. 20–30)

In a flatter descriptive vein, Wordsworth notes the rock-foliage and a mountain-cottage visible above and beyond the dell; then he turns without transition to a voice even more discursive:

> I gazed and gazed, and to myself I said
> 'Our thoughts at least are ours; and this wild nook,
> My EMMA, I will dedicate to thee'.

Yet the gesture of naming hardly resolves the intensity of tranced gazing, nor does it give a clue to the rationale or tone of the previous thirty-six lines of presumably meaningful description. Perhaps there is a suppressed context of affection between the speaker and Emma (in still another obliquity, Dorothy is given a pseudonym). Some such emotion presumably composes the details and provokes the defensive 'Our thoughts at least are ours' as the mind's resistance to the external scene. But beyond the general or emblematic connection of Emma with springtime freshness we cannot know.

In the splendid 'Nutting' of a year earlier (1798), Wordsworth's solemn meditative tone is contradicted by the quality and nature of the experience described. The fragment begins with a false start:

> —————————. . . It seems a day
> (I speak of one from many singled out)
> One of those heavenly days that cannot die. . . .

Out of the undifferentiated sea of memory he singles this day as 'heavenly'. Perhaps it is because he is so intrepid, for once potently managing his environment:

> O'er path-less rocks,
> Through beds of matted fern, and tangled thickets,
> Forcing my way, I came to one dear nook
> Unvisited, where not a broken bough
> Drooped with its withered leaves, ungracious sign
> Of devastation; but the hazels rose
> Tall and erect, with tempting clusters hung,
> A virgin scene!

After a long pause when with voluptuous restraint he 'eyed/The Banquet' in the security of deep joy, the child desecrates and rapes the the trees. The language of sexual violation is Wordsworth's:

Then up I rose,
And dragged to earth both branch and bough, with crash
And merciless ravage: and the shady nook
Of hazels, and the green and mossy bower,
Deformed and sullied, patiently gave up
Their quiet being. . . .

Neither the fleeting 'sense of pain' he records, nor the final three
lines:

Then, dearest Maiden, move along these shades
In gentleness of heart; with gentle hand
Touch — for there is a spirit in the woods,

can impugn the wisdom of the accumulated images which reveal
him as, in isolated seclusion, the exulting destroyer of non-human
nature.

Picturesque and beautiful nature Wordsworth can often manage;
but in many vivid episodes of exposure on crag and moor, sublime
nature manages him. 'Nutting' describes a picturesque or beautiful
ideal, the phase of 'heavenly' consummation most devoutly to be
wished in Wordsworth's 'spousal verse'. The poem represents an
extreme, not just marriage but deliberate rape, landscape passively
giving up to his possession its 'quiet being' while he remains safe
from the threat of a rival or access of self-consciousness. Rather
similarly, the *Poems on the Naming of Places* appropriate scenes by naming
them. For this humanizing process, certain scenes are better than
others: Wordsworth's love for nooks and protected valleys, for
instance, largely derives from his belief that some kinds of terrain are
more tractable, more easily personified. This is true of the 'wild secluded scene' of the Wye Valley, whose cliffs 'impress/Thoughts of
more deep seclusion'; and true as well of the deep Vale of Grasmere,
'the calmest, fairest spot on earth' with its embracing hills. The
dwelling of the Solitary in *The Excursion* is a similar but smaller
'sweet recess' in the mountains: 'Urn-like it was in shape, deep as an
urn;/With rocks encompassed. . . . A quiet treeless nook'; but here,
Wordsworth has hardly said 'peace is here/Or nowhere' when he and
the Wanderer encounter a rural funeral and with it the disillusioned
Solitary, who in his person contradicts the quiet of the visible
Vale.

Perhaps the loveliest of the images of seclusion is *The Prelude*
description of Furness Abbey in the Vale of Nightshade. Wordsworth

explains that when young he and his friends would rent horses and
visit the Druid's Circle at Swinside above the lower Duddon River;
or they would ride twenty-one miles and visit

> the antique walls
> Of that large abbey, where within the Vale
> Of Nightshade, to St. Mary's honour built,
> Stands yet a mouldering pile with fractured arch,
> Belfry, and images, and living trees,
> A holy scene! Along the smooth green turf
> Our horses grazed. To more than inland peace
> Left by the west wind sweeping overhead
> From a tumultuous ocean, trees and towers
> In that sequestered valley may be seen,
> Both silent and both motionless alike;
> Such the deep shelter that is there, and such
> The safeguard for repose and quietness.
>
> (II, ll. 102–14)

The assimilation of the trees – the adjective 'living' shocks with its
apt simplicity – to the inanimate ruin, and the towers to the trees,
'Both silent and both motionless alike', could hardly be more subtle
in expressing through the visible landscape a wish for the permanence
of which Furness Abbey, like Tintern, is the continuing reminder.

Even the mock-heroic frame concerned with boyhood sports,
which surrounds and prepares these perceptions of 'deep shelter', has
its use and relevance as an indication that these images mean even
more to the mature poet than they did to the experiencing child.

> Our steeds remounted and the summons given,
> With whip and spur we through the chauntry flew
> In uncouth race, and left the cross-legged knight,
> And the stone abbot, and that single wren
> Which one day sang so sweetly in the nave
> Of the old church, that – though from recent showers
> The earth was comfortless, and touched by faint
> Internal breezes, sobbings of the place
> And respirations, from the roofless walls
> The shuddering ivy dripped large drops – yet still
> So sweetly 'mid the gloom the invisible bird
> Sang to herself, that there I could have made

70

My dwelling-place, and lived for ever there
To hear such music. Through the walls we flew
And down the valley, and, a circuit made
In wantonness of heart, through rough and smooth
We scampered homewards.

(II, 115–31)

One voice gives way to another, more impassioned voice in the midst of a catalogue, the explicit instance of 'that single wren/Which one day' sang unleashing an intensely empathic description which usurps and extends the long sentence, exhausting the full meaning of the example for the mature poet. The 'faint/Internal breezes' sob and respire humanly, animating the protected enclosure while the sea wind sweeps overhead in the outside world. The unseen wren singing 'to herself' completes the animation, so much an evidence of life in perfect safety for the bird, as poet's surrogate, 'that there I could have made/My dwelling-place, and lived for ever there' to make and hear such music. The phrasing 'could have made' is tentative, but in comparison with the final lines of Hardy's 'Darkling Thrush',

> . . . I could think there trembled through
> His happy good-night air
> Some blessed Hope, whereof he knew
> And I was unaware,

Wordsworth's attribution is generously and unguardedly made.

About 1840, before the Kendal and Windermere Railway was built to run alongside Furness Abbey and ruin its associations, Wordsworth wrote a tame descriptive sonnet on the place. The account is far inferior to that in *The Prelude* but illustrates his love of the assimilation of architecture to nature. It begins:

> Here, where, of havoc tired and rash undoing,
> Man left this Structure to become Time's prey,
> A soothing spirit follows in the way
> That Nature takes, her counter-work pursuing.
> See how her Ivy clasps the sacred Ruin,
> Fall to prevent or beautify decay;
> And, on the mouldered walls, how bright, how gay,
> The flowers in pearly dews their bloom renewing!

Nature regains her own by an infinite plenitude and patience. The recognition is very explicit later in life when Wordsworth, writing more about humanized man and about buildings in nature, finds comfort in the idea of perpetual renewal, an order which reaches beyond individual death. But if he had consciously foreseen how nature would replenish her ravaged hazel boughs the poem 'Nutting' would never have been written, the pleasure of his role as destroyer of nature being negated by remembrance of his own death and the boundless patience and continually renewed life of natural forms.

In Wordsworth, landscape feeling undergoes a difficult passage to ethical consciousness, fastening on the combined exposure and seclusion of buildings which makes them emblems, not only of mind in world, but perhaps also of self in society. Tintern and Furness Abbeys, Bolton Priory in 'The White Doe', King's College Chapel in a late sonnet, are ecclesiastical buildings or ruins which Wordsworth chooses as the setting of formative secular experiences apprehended with a religious intensity. When, in the Vale of Nightshade, he describes the motionless trees and towers and remarks 'A holy scene!' the reference is not to the abbey but to the emotional import of its naturalized ruin; and when he describes Trinity Chapel, Cambridge, the single remembrance is a thought of Newton's statue

> with his prism and silent face,
> The marble image of a mind for ever
> Voyaging through strange seas of thought, alone.

Wordsworth praises Peele Castle and Kilchurn Castle for their obdurate endurance, for remaining intact beyond their historical 'infancy'. He addresses Kilchurn as the 'Child of loud-throated War', and in a magnificent, sophisticated image of seclusion he ends his tribute by a form of unwitty landscape pun in the metaphysical equation of time and space:

> Shade of departed Power
> Skeleton of unfleshed humanity,
> The chronicle were welcome that should call
> Into the compass of distinct regard
> The toils and struggles of thy infant years!
> Yon foaming flood seems motionless as ice;
> Its dizzy turbulence eludes the eye,
> Frozen by distance; so, majestic Pile,
> To the perception of this Age, appear

Thy fierce beginnings, softened and subdued
And quieted in character – the strife,
The pride, the fury uncontrollable,
Lost on the aërial heights of the Crusades!

The wonder and use of a ruin is that it reminds the observer of by-gone human strife, pride, and fury; representing the past in the present, it is analogous to a poem on emotions recollected in tranquillity.

Humbler ruins like the unfinished sheepfold which is the focus of the poem 'Michael' (1800), or the ruined cottage whose condition is the register of Margaret's grief in Book I of *The Excursion*, are even more approachable as the 'image of tranquillity' amidst the common-place. In an imagined 'Address From the Spirit of Cockermouth Castle', Wordsworth refers to the dark castle dungeon as a 'tutor' which made his 'young thoughts acquainted with the grave'; and in *The Prelude* he speaks of the less imposing but no less real 'ministra-tion' of the 'lowly cottages' of his youth. In fact, sometimes Words-worth's love for Lake District cottages – expressed in 'Home at Grasmere', the early books of *The Prelude*, and in considerable detail in *Guide to the Lakes* – may seem even more compelling than his Immor-tality Ode account of 'that imperial palace' from which the earth slowly alienates 'her Foster-child, her Inmate Man'. Yet these and other images of joyous place-affection, arising from his wish for rooted moral meditation and for the 'calm' which he always associ-ated with profound feelings of joy, tend to value states of being at one with a scene rather than distinct from it. To the extent that they do so without qualification they lose what William James would call the 'bracing' effect of recognizing the otherness of the external world. What Wordsworth never makes explicit is his belief that the self should find its nook in the social world just as the mind discovers itself 'exquisitely fitted' to the world of objects and external pre-sences. He rarely saw that place, which should be the natural transi-tion from epistemology to ethics, can be instead a retreat from the question; that the premise of solitude, more like suffering than action, can become stasis.

3

Coleridge in *Table Talk* called Wordsworth a *spectator ab extra* on man and nature. This becomes workable once we qualify it by remarking that finally Wordsworth is a man who knows that other persons, like the landscape, exist outside the self; and that he continually seeks to disprove this knowledge by recording and interpreting instances of transcendence. The disillusionment that all his best poems convey is the final impossibility of a lasting and absolute relation between mind and world where limits are abolished. His checks on his preconceptions are at such times wonderfully alert. This is the centre of Wordsworth's greatness, an honesty about secular experience, a nontranscendent image of man as man that goes no further than reasonable optimism about life on earth, which every excellent poet of the century learned directly or indirectly from him. Certainly Thomas Hardy often begins in poems and novels where Wordsworth left off, making this facet of Wordsworth one of his main speculative concerns, eagerly on the watch for a transcendence he can honestly permit.

To recapitulate: Wordsworth did not see clearly how the role of the philosophical poet, with its inevitable seclusion and strategic retreat, can constrict a poetry which begins in sensuous, specific experience in the world. Because of the nature of his hopes and fears the meditative tendency, present from the start in his poetry and salutary in many cases, begins to over-compensate especially after his brother's death in 1805. Wordsworth himself, according to Ernest de Selincourt, 'recognized only one point of cleavage in the continuity of his poetic life: he dated it from his residence at Alfoxden (1797–8). Poems written before this time he regarded as JUVENILIA, and such as he deemed worthy of publication he largely recast.' Yet the early 1790s were, after all, the years when he somehow taught himself to be a poet; and along with *The Borderers* there are a few poems of this period, largely unretouched, which prepare for that point of cleavage. One poem in particular has much to say against deliberate seclusion as a human expedient.

The prolix title, lengthy and descriptive like the full title of 'Tintern Abbey', suggests this poem's open-ended construction: 'Lines left upon a Seat in a Yew-Tree, which stands near the Lake of Esthwaite, on a Desolate part of the Shore, commanding a Beautiful

Prospect.' 'Lines' only, not stanzaic, and as it were a set of spontaneous orderings, not even 'verses'. 'Beautiful' and 'prospect', eighteenth-century terms for aspects of landscape, are drawn upon here for the basic contrast of the poem as Wordsworth stresses the difference between the desolate foreground and the overpowering beauty of the distant panorama:

> — Stranger! these gloomy boughs
> Had charms for him; and here he loved to sit,
> His only visitants a straggling sheep,
> The stone-chat, or the glancing sand-piper:
> And on these barren rocks, with fern and heath,
> And juniper and thistle, sprinkled o'er,
> Fixing his downcast eye, he many an hour
> A morbid pleasure nourished, tracing here
> An emblem of his own unfruitful life. . . .

This man, 'Fixing his downcast eye', is the first of Wordsworth's sceptical solitaries, men unlike the beggar and leech gatherer because they deliberately exile themselves from the human circle.

Wordsworth himself, tough-minded in his condemnation, sees this man's construction of the bower on the barren place as a deliberate self-laceration, the deepest kind of injury, a cutting-off from human society. The solitary here delights in the melancholy of the contrast and traces emblems in the outer landscape of his own mental desolation. He is as it were reduced to landscape from society. Near-by, his only 'visitants' are sheep, birds: a lesser contact and an inadequate solace. Ironically that beautiful prospect is not society either, but simply a more humanly manageable landscape.

Rarely has Wordsworth written a poem which so forcibly demonstrates the inadequacy of landscape — at any rate the picturesque and beautiful ideas of landscape. He affirms in fact a true and completer landscape which is the same as nature itself. Using the example of a person who has lost connection, he shows the dangers of solipsism and the sentimental manipulation of the scene. The point is that landscape is landscape because it is finally other, inhuman. It must remain distant. But Nature is a more encompassing ideal, swallowing all divisions and labels, permitting man to conceive himself in innumerable relations with a world of which he considers himself a part.

By the most plausible transition, in lines immediately following those quoted above, Wordworth conveys his contrast not theoretically but by the movement of his character's eyes upwards:

And, lifting up his head, he then would gaze
On the more distant scene, – how lovely 'tis
Thou seest, – and he would gaze till it became
Far lovelier, and his heart could not sustain
The beauty, still more beauteous! Nor, that time,
When nature had subdued him to herself,
Would he forget those Beings to whose minds
Warm from the labours of benevolence
The world, and human life, appeared a scene
Of kindred loveliness: then he would sigh,
Inly disturbed, to think that others felt
What he must never feel: and so, lost Man!
On visionary views would fancy feed,
Till his eye streamed with tears.

The gap is between outer loveliness and the solitary's inward, barren landscape of despair. The passage recreates the psychological process of false response, beginning with the repetition of the focal words 'gaze', 'lovely', 'beauty'. From the man's self-condemnation the passage moves to the fanciful 'visionary views' which have no connection with what he sees with his outer eyes, streaming as they are with tears. Landscape is here not enough for solace: when used by deranged sensibility for escape it merely mocks the observer. Only when the repeated intense gazing and gazing is the action of healthy sensibility as it is in a poem like 'I wandered lonely as a cloud', does it create legitimate joy in the observer: only in the healthy sensibility is the inward eye 'the bliss of solitude'.

Wordsworth is so concerned with the direct moral impact of the poem's message, so concerned to involve the reader in the circumstances of the situation, that he fabricates the dramatic situation of the pretended address at the sight of the bower: the 'lines left upon a seat' which beckon the reader-traveller to rest even though the spot is 'Far from all human dwelling'. In the passage just quoted he speaks in an unexpected aside to the reader, calling attention to the visible scene; finally, cutting his landscape-anecdote short because he intends a very stark and sudden contrast between the man alive and the man dead, he abdicates the pretence at narrative, concluding his description of impassioned ecstasy very flatly: 'In this deep vale/ He died, – this seat his only monument.' The tone of the moral exemplum and the archaic address 'Stranger!' suggest that Wordsworth intends his own poem to be a 'monument' in the sense so often referred to in other poems and in his 'Essay on Epitaphs', where a man's life or a moment of experience is summed up briefly for incisive preservation to posterity. The epitaph or monument is thus at once elegiac and educative, commemorating the dead person or the lapsed experience, and teaching the living how to live.

In such a scheme, from the outset the didactic intention is never missing. Since the poet's ability to generalize from the particular is of primary importance, simple descriptive data is not enough. Wordsworth here uses a highly schematic narrative method, yet narrative is not his main objective: if it had been he would have ended 'In this deep vale he died'. The lines which remain are very direct confrontations of the educative implications of the elegiac landscape opening. They clarify by sheer statement the charged language of the landscape descriptions, putting into relief the contrast between 'true knowledge' and its opposite. Then the poem simply, at mid-line, stops – a fragment of experience which does not bother to fill in the exact requirements of an external form. Even the abrupt ending is part of the intended spontaneity of effect.

Wordsworth had the idea for the poem by 1787 at Hawkshead and he may even have written out a version of the anecdotal material at that time. Yet surely the last seventeen lines are later work, development of the implications of his anecdote, a generalizing away from the instance couched now in the language of imagination, animism, and faculties which he was to use with strength of philosophical reference in the next decade.

> If Thou be one whose heart the holy forms
> Of young imagination have kept pure,
> Stranger! henceforth be warned; and know that pride,
> Howe'er disguised in its own majesty,
> Is littleness; that he who feels contempt
> For any living thing, hath faculties
> Which he has never used; that thought with him
> Is in its infancy. . . .
>   O be wiser, Thou!
> Instructed that true knowledge leads to love. . . .

Granted the dramatic situation, the imagined immediacy, this openly didactic ending yet does not derive from an impulse entirely separate from the subtly moralized landscape of the opening two–thirds of the poem. Rather, the poem prefigures the writing of 'Tintern Abbey' and The Prelude in its controlled, deliberate movement

from description to relevant meditation, in its reverence for those
'holy forms/Of young imagination', and in the assertion of a frame
of mind, between self-suspicion and self-confidence, where greatness
is possible. Wordsworth moves, with only a slight sense of disconnection, from one mode of the mind to another. Only a short time
later, in 'Tintern Abbey', he was able to make impassioned transitions between description and meditation, blendings of both modes
back and forth in the same poem, infusing one mode with the other,
energizing general statements with selected details and evolving a
non-metaphorical language which, by a density of repeated terms
and cross-references, presented a simulacrum of the flux and reflux of
the mind.

What points ahead in particular is the delicate animism of lines
like

> . . . this aged tree
> With its dark arms,

or

> His only visitants a straggling sheep,
> The stone-chat, or the glancing sand-piper,

or, conclusively,

> . . . he, who feels contempt
> For any living thing, hath faculties
> Which he has never used.

Such lines show that Wordworth has by 1797 disembarrassed himself
of the formal simile and detachable detail of his early poems in
couplets. Perhaps by self-schooling with Shakespeare in *The Borderers*
he learned the flexibility and intensity of blank verse for the transitions he wanted, the artless rhetoric he believed capable of conveying
intense emotion with clarity. The simplicity of his developed means
of expression reveals a heightened sophistication arrived at almost
overnight between 1793–7. Now he has determined to vivify and
deepen the topographical landscape genre by descriptive, meditative,
and narrative elements—by these three in any combination or in
concert.

4

For the first time in Wordsworth's career, 'Lines left upon a Seat'
presents illustration and enactment of that 'true knowledge' which is
the centre of all his later epistemology. Such knowledge 'leads to
love' because it means relation, connection, a belief in human
solidarity, the defeat of the isolate self in the willingness to give.
Knowledge of this sort is of a relation with nature and with mankind: a relation which, because it presupposes the poet's mind both
register and possessor of the two, must persistently take into
account that 'pride . . . is littleness' and separates man from nature.
Since such relation means the engagement of the full emotional and
intellectual man, Wordsworth's condemnation of someone who has
'faculties/Which he has never used' is most serious, foreshadowing
his anger at the use of 'reason's knife' by the French rationalists of
the Terror. Later on, in his Poetical Works, his arrangement of poems
by 'faculties' or states of life which were at the same time genres,
shows a related intention to demonstrate by ascending sequence the
picture of a full mind. However he did not realize how in fact such a
division would only make the presiding intellect of the poems taken
as a whole seem portionable, divisible. Similarly, *The Prelude's* Snowdon vision and *The Excursion's* fiery sunset 'Repeated; but with unity
sublime' in the mirroring lake, are not so much encountered in the
respective final books of these poems, as manipulated into place for
elevating, emblematic flourishes.

In 'Tintern Abbey' and the early books of *The Prelude* Wordsworth
proves himself

> . . . well pleased to recognize
> In nature and the language of the sense
> The anchor of my purest thoughts, the nurse,
> The guide, the guardian of my heart, and soul
> Of all my moral being.

But in the later *Prelude* by an unconscious reverse of these figures of
the mind as patient, follower, and ward, the mind is called 'lord and
master', with 'outward sense/The obedient servant of her will' (XII,
11. 222–3). As if the discipline of his early landscape poems was in
no sense a moral discipline, Wordsworth increasingly wished to
humanize poetry that was already human. Nevertheless this honest

attempt to extend his convictions, and to write a more comprehensive poetry than the kind he wrote in his twenties, was an inevitable
strengthening of the moral emphases present in his best early poems.
He was trying to write the kind of poetry appropriate to his time of
life, and it was characteristic of his 'Egotistical Sublime' that he
could not abandon the premise of landscape for another focus but
felt committed to moralize it in terms of emblems and types.

The notion of the educative value of landscape best explains the
gradual transition from landscape to ethics. Despite Wordsworth's
own yoking of beauty and fear as tandem influences in the outer
world, in *The Prelude* the most formative landscape effects are in fact
those of greatness, peril, and infinity – images of exposure, particularly among the mountains:

> Attention comes,
> And comprehensiveness and memory,
> From early converse with the works of God
> Among all regions; chiefly where appear
> Most obviously simplicity and power.
> By influence habitual to the mind
> The mountain's outline and its steady form
> Gives a pure grandeur, and its presence shapes
> The measure and the prospect of the soul
> To majesty; such virtue have the forms
> Perennial of the ancient hills; nor less
> The changeful language of their countenances
> Gives movement to the thoughts, and multitude,
> With order and relation.
>
> (1805, VII, ll. 716–29)

According to Wordsworth the lines from consciousness to con-
science may be traced by reference to the sublimity of non-human
nature. Fear more than domestic beauty is a fostering emotion
because it confronts the mind with mighty forms. Norman Lacey
rightly says Wordsworth 'feels awe, almost terror, before the Grandeur of Nature, but his feeling takes on the greatness of that which
inspires it, so that his pain and fear are ennobled, and the adventure
of human life is raised in dignity by the grandeur of its setting'
(*Wordsworth's View of Nature*, 1948). Thus Wordsworth makes a point
of claiming that it is the 'undersense of greatest' and memory of the
mountains which preserve him from the distractions of London.

When sublime forms of nature lead the poet to conceive the

greatness of his own powers, they amplify his image of man. Accordingly, Wordsworth emphasizes the concept of 'leading' as the original meaning of education. In 'Tintern Abbey', for instance, he describes 'that serene and blessed mood/In which the affections gently lead us on' and the privilege of Nature 'to lead/From joy to joy'. And, when he recounts the boat-stealing episode in *The Prelude*, his reference to Nature (with a feminine personal pronoun) is offhand and parenthetical, but determines the whole tone of the description and the ensuing account of 'unknown modes of being': 'One summer evening (led by her) I found/A little boat tied to a willow tree...' (I, 1. 357 f.). The passage quoted above on the moral and intellectual influence of mountain terrain (1805, VII, 1. 716 f.) is characteristic of this whole tendency, for there Wordsworth, describing the forms which have shaped his own mind, so minimizes the differences between descriptive and prescriptive statement that he seems to be outlining the ideal moral education for others as well. His self-congratulation on this score is most evident when he compares himself with Coleridge:

> Thou, my Friend! wert reared
> In the great city, 'mid far other scenes;
> But we, by different roads, at length have gained
> The self-same bourne.
>
> (II, 11. 451–4)
>
> I did not pine like one in cities bred,
> As was thy melancholy lot, dear Friend!
> Great Spirit as thou art, in endless dreams
> Of sickliness, disjoining, joining, things
> Without the light of knowledge.
>
> (VIII, 11. 433–7)

Throughout his letters and poems Wordsworth's hope is that by the 'regular action of the world' habits will be produced which will lead to the moral life; such habits of meditation are his way of discovering the 'moral relations' under which his poetry can subsume the 'most ordinary appearances' of the material universe. But he does not fully perceive the anomaly that Coleridge arrived at the 'self-same bourne' after his youth was past and by another road; and rather similarly he traces the rise of sympathy with man and nature in the reprobate hero of his tale 'Peter Bell' (1798), but he never initially explains how Peter has arrived at manhood untouched and untaught by nature.

We cannot, however, press too hard on what may seem obvious self-contradictions in external narrative, for sometimes Wordsworth permits himself gaps in verisimilitude and logical coherence in the intensity of working out ontological statements. In his *Prelude* account of how the forms of nature do and should lead to habits of thinking, associating, and meditating, he is interested in the process of tutorial by nature, fully aware that emotion regularized into habit is no longer spontaneous. Yet he is, as he knows, fully justified in schematizing or even suppressing part of that knowledge when he is recreating the process of personal growth.

5

Often, what Wordsworth means to say is plain enough and easily paraphrasable; he does in fact prosecute an argument in the ordinary way with principles, instances, digressions; yet it is also plain that often the poetry does not succeed wholly in carrying the meaning live into the heart (to quote his own great phrase). Only when he claims more than he shows may we suspect his lack of integration. There is no more crucial spot for testing this than in the place, dead centre in the poem on the growth of his own mind, where he professes to document the regretful but eminently human change from sensing to writing. Wordsworth in Book VIII of *The Prelude* seems to have meant 'Retrospect: Love of Nature Leading to Love of Man' as a putative solution to the major transition in the growth of the poetic mind. Not entirely by admission, it is an imperfect solution because remembered, conjectural, and highly selective; it is the poem's solution but it is not necessarily Wordsworth's own full solution. If this is true the title of the book is somewhat misleading, a possible ideal phrased in the continuing present ('Leading') rather than an accomplished fact. Book VIII, as becomes clear, is in the nature of a formal justification, almost a revision of the earlier books done to fill gaps and strengthen the argument concerning imaginative sympathy with man. In the first lines of Book IX, Wordsworth says the just-completed Book VIII resembles a river that loops back over regions already crossed in an attempt to avoid being engulfed in the 'ravenous sea'; or it is like a traveller on a high prospect scanning from 'the brow/Of some aerial Down' a region he has passed and striving 'from that height, with one and yet one more/Last look, to make the best amends he may'. Books IX and following, he implies, are of an entirely different sort, 'Oh, how much unlike the past!'

Book VIII presents neither landscape nor its critique. Landscape is instead, as it were, drawn back into the concept of Nature which is its parent or of which it is the visible sign; while individual men are effortlessly seen as archetypal Man – in this case the 'condition' of the Shepherd, for 'Shepherds were the men that pleased me first' (1. 128). This is the significance of the amazing peopled landscape at the outset of the book where Wordsworth enters the consciousness of high Helvellyn and apprehends a 'rustic fair' from the mountain's perspective. The 'little family' of men are joyous in their 'secluded glen' – the solitary mountain looms exposed with his 'unshrouded head':

> What sounds are those, Helvellyn, that are heard
> Up to thy summit, through the depth of air
> Ascending, as if distance had the power
> To make the sounds more audible? What crowd
> Covers, or sprinkles o'er, yon village green?
> Crowd seems it, solitary hill! to thee,
> Though but a little family of men,
> Shepherds and tillers of the ground. . . .
>
> (11. 1–8)

'Sprinkles' gives some sense of the vast perspective Wordsworth is assuming as his own. He moves as by a magnifying lens close for a description of the throng of hawkers, Dalesmen, wives and children, in the mode of fancy, then back again to an olympian perspective:

> – Immense
> Is the recess, the circumambient world
> Magnificent, by which they are embraced:

The mountain folk

> Through utter weakness pitiably dear,
> As tender infants are: and yet how great!

When he speaks in this way, Wordsworth cannot help sounding a little foolish. Yet the overstatement is so consistent, so sincere, that he almost compels assent.

No other major writer of his century would have ventured that final phrase about men as 'tender infants' who are none the less 'great'; nor the unguarded affirmations which follow:

83   G

For all things serve them: them the morning light
Loves, as it glistens on the silent rocks;
And them the silent rocks, which now from high
Look down upon them; the reposing clouds;
The wild brooks prattling from invisible haunts;
And old Helvellyn, conscious of the stir
Which animates this day their calm abode.

(cf. 11. 55–69)

Wordsworth writes in a magniloquent style with Miltonic syntax when he treats of the 'circumambient world', but in a flat narrative tone when he treats the figures in the scene; in the 1850 recension he even relaxes his idiom to quote five pedestrian lines from Joseph Cottle (11. 48–52). The gap between these languages of imagination and fancy, the rapid changes in focus, the final loving reference to the consciousness of Helvellyn hardly serve to unify character and environment. One is left with the sense that the magnificent embracing scene, with its composing presence of 'old Helvellyn', has condescended to patronize humanity – just this once on the annual festival when the atmospheric conditions are propitious.

Wordsworth says Helvellyn loves and approves the people in their 'secluded glen' below, but the distance remains – literal and figurative. We are reminded of the splendid portrait of 'Wordsworth on Helvellyn' by B. R. Haydon, which pictures the old poet with his craggy nose, brooding as he gazes downward, with a background of storm and charging mists. Haydon remarks in Wordsworth this characteristic reluctance to share or dissipate a poetic isolation when he describes a time in London when he

> was walking with him in Pall Mall; we darted into Chrystie's. A copy of the 'transfiguration' was at the head of the room, and in the corner a beautiful copy of the 'Cupid and Psyche' (statues) kissing. . . . You remember this exquisite group? . . . Catching sight of the Cupid . . . Wordsworth's face reddened, he showed his teeth, and then said in a loud voice 'THE DEV-V-V-ILS!' There's a mind! Ought not this exquisite group have roused his 'Shapes of Beauty', and have softened his heart as much as his old grey-mossed rocks, his withered thorn, and his dribbling mountain streams?

(Journals, ed. W. B. Pope, 1964, II, 470)

Haydon as the average sensual man dislikes Wordsworth's 'selfish Quakerism, his affection of superior virtue; his utter insensibility to the frailties – the beautiful frailties of passion'. Though Haydon perhaps in part speaks out of jealousy for Wordsworth's sternness and his reputation, neither of which he possessed himself, his noticing that the poet loves grey-mossed rocks rather than the naked human figure points to a whole sector of human experience the landscape poet leaves virtually untouched.

Certainly Wordsworth's feeling of kinship with the solitary mountain and its exposed elevation, announced at the beginning of Book VIII, stands as an unconscious check to anything which approaches a full leading to the love of man. But the importance of this introduction to the book is that Wordsworth, wrongly feeling the human image in the first books of the poem is not plain or human enough, but requiring a way into the experience of revolutionary France in the following books, attempts to stretch landscape into a coexistence with society. In this case it is the manageable society of the 'family' of Dalesmen grouped at the fair, but however rudimentary, it is nevertheless the first genuine picture of community in *The Prelude*. The poet's grammar school with its interludes of gregarious sport, Cambridge, and London are not presented as true community but as in effect successively more serious impediments to another kind of communion – with the forms of nature. Book VIII falls short in trying to reverse this direction, but the attempt is serious, intelligent, and in its way compelling because it is as if Wordsworth, knowing what a large concession he is making to the rational side of the mind, struggles against his reluctance to jettison landscape. This explains why the book is the most disorganized of all, with more special pleading and lapses of tone ('Alas! I feel/That I am triffling'), and with a great many 1850 revisions and cuts.

Particularly in the decade 1800–10, Wordsworth's concern with community was never far from mind. In January 1801 he wrote to Charles James Fox praising the property-owning 'Statesmen' of Cumberland and noting that 'The Brothers' and 'Michael' were written to show that men 'who do not wear fine cloaths can feel deeply'; in June 1802 he discusses in a related letter, among other topics, 'the influence of natural objects in forming character' in men and nations, a subject taken up again in his 'Letter to Mathetes' in *The Friend* (1809). The tone of these prose statements does not differ much from his praise of shepherds and Dalesmen in Book

VIII, where nature is as ever 'a gracious Guide, to lead . . . forth/
Beyond the bosom of . . . Family,/. . . Friends and youthful playmates'
to a human love for 'the Creature in himself/As he appear'd, a
stranger in my path' (1805 version). In a revealing inconsistency
Wordsworth says the shepherds he knew, the men that pleased him
first, were not like Arcadian shepherds of the Golden Age nor like
those in Spenser or in Shakespeare's Arden Forest; they were
ordinary men, he claims, 'intent on little but substantial needs' (1.
129 f.). Yet a hundred lines later, naturalizing the English shepherd
in the 'awful solitudes' of a sublime terrain, the occupation is
idealized in another, equally falsifying way by the young poet. The
claims are large indeed:

> Philosophy, methinks, at Fancy's call,
> Might deign to follow him. . . .
>   A rambling school-boy, thus
> I felt his presence in his own domain,
> As of a lord and master, or a power,
> Or genius, under Nature, under God,
> Presiding; and severest solitude
> Had more commanding looks when he was there.
> (cf. 11. 249–61)

Wordsworth looks exclusively at the shepherd's association with
mountain solitude; and this instance of sublimity, described in
terms of the fostering fear which pervades the visionary episodes of
Books I and II, is his deliberate reduction to show how 'men before
my inexperienced eyes/Did first present themselves purified,/
Removed, and to a distance that was fit'.

The reconstruction of childhood perception of the shepherd in
landscape is Wordsworth's instance of how 'we all of us in some
degree/Are led to knowledge'. But though it is well qualified by his
adult recognition that shepherds are ordinary men, somehow the full
account is less than convincing as an explanation of the origins of
human sympathy. The passage in question is the visionary heart of
Book VIII:

> When up the lonely brooks on rainy days
> Angling I went, or trod the trackless hills
> By mists bewildered, suddenly mine eyes
> Have glanced upon him distant a few steps,
> In size a giant, stalking through thick fog,

His sheep like Greenland bears; or, as he stepped
Beyond the boundary line of some hill-shadow,
His form hath flashed upon me, glorified
By the deep radiance of the setting sun:
Or him have I descried in distant sky,
A solitary object and sublime,
Above all height! like an aerial cross
Stationed alone upon a spiry rock
Of the Chartreuse, for worship.

(11. 262–75)

Wordsworth says he 'first . . . looked/At Man through objects that
were great or fair;/First communed with him by their help', thus
having a 'prepossession' of his genuine insight into humanity, once
again knowing a truth before experiencing it because imagination
treats as prelusive the symbolic suggestions of nature. Yet it is necessary to note how relentlessly sublime and awesome are his focal
images of shepherds: 'In size a giant', 'glorified', 'Above all height',
'Stationed alone . . . for worship'. It is possible to doubt whether in
fact a full image of man can be mediated by way of the sublime
alone. Here the movement is from a genuine perception of the man
'distant a few steps' to a solitary 'object' (the word is significant)
'Above all height'. As John Jones says, there is a loss of command,
a confusion, so that Wordsworth's 'final unlucky reference to the
Cross is a cry for help, in work which his poetry cannot do alone'.
And, following after this descriptive passage, Wordsworth uses
the hasty 'thus' and 'hence' which often cover his difficulties
in these later books: 'Thus was man/Ennobled outwardly before
my sight', 'hence the human form/To me became an index of
delight'.

When he discusses Cambridge and London in the last two
hundred lines of the book, he returns to and reinforces his earlier
treatment, adding the chiaroscuro of deepened perception of human
suffering but leaving unchanged the lineaments of the imagination's
antagonism to urban community present in Books III and VII. He
criticizes Cambridge and London, and romantic pastoral, in terms of
their unreality, their distance from what he calls the 'ordinary
interests of mankind'. The result, as David Ferry says, is paradoxical
for both Wordsworth and the reader, because in the profoundest
sense 'the ordinary interests of man are for Wordsworth those which
carry him furthest from the world of social experience'. The poem

87

'Michael' is a larger and more adequate solution because it is packed with commonplace detail and employs narrative and meditative modes to give meaningful sequence; but even there Wordsworth makes feeling as affection for property and family the peasant's deepest emotion, reserving imaginative feeling for himself. His interest in rural people connects him through George Eliot and William Barnes with Hardy and D. H. Lawrence; but the novelists deal with particular people in the round as figures of tragic possibility.

We may, I think, describe the true allegiance of Book VIII by briefly examining Wordsworth's debt to Milton. The Miltonic vocabulary and syntax of 'the circumambient world/Magnificent' has already been discussed as the key to Wordsworth's indecisive response to the rural fair; but if I am right Milton everywhere comes to the surface of this book when Wordsworth is verging closest on his deepest yearnings. Early in the book Wordsworth compares Gehol's matchless gardens with 'the paradise/Where I was reared', in a passage following *Paradise Lost*, Book IV, lines 208–47. As Milton dismisses scenes from history and fiction in comparison with Eden, Wordsworth rejects a beautifully composed Chinese garden scene in favour of 'the common haunts of the green earth' in Cumberland, not here Eden but 'paradise' itself. A similar love of place and its associations informs the descriptions of Helvellyn, of the 'Moors, mountains, headlands, and . . . hollow vales' of northern England (1. 215 f.), and of a memorable sunset on Thurston-mere which rouses Wordsworth to yet another tribute to his 'Dear native Regions' (1. 458 f.). But in the 'busy hum' of London, human nature 'was not a punctual presence' (see *Paradise Lost*, VIII, 23: 'This punctual spot'), confined to specific place, 'but a spirit/Diffused through time and space, with aid derived/From monuments' and from books: it was thus a less immediate and affecting emotion than love of place. He was 'seeking knowledge at that time/Far less than craving power', though the whole brunt of his landscape imagery is a disparagement of knowledge and a hunger for power as he defines it.

At the end of Book VIII, an image seems to summarize the debt to Milton, and indeed the whole *Prelude*, in its brilliance and confusion. Wordsworth is discussing how his 'young imagination' acclimated itself to suffering and evil in the city, how vice, guilt, debasement and misery could not overthrow his trust 'in what we may become' (see *Paradise Lost*, XI, 204 f.):

From those sad scenes when meditation turned,
Lo! every thing that was indeed divine
Retained its purity inviolate,
Nay brighter shone, by this portentous gloom
Set off; such opposition as aroused
The mind of Adam, yet in Paradise
Though fallen from bliss, when in the East he saw
Darkness ere day's mid course, and morning light
More orient in the western cloud, that drew
O'er the blue firmament a radiant white,
Descending slow with something heavenly fraught.

(11. 654–64)

It is a magnificently relevant piece of literary plundering, and the description of not merely Adam but the mind of Adam 'yet in paradise/Though fallen from bliss', is not the unconscious or chance phrasing of this poet's poem about the adequacy of landscape.

6

When Arthur Hallam in his review of Tennyson's first volume of poems (*The Englishman's Magazine*, 1831) defended Tennyson as, like Keats, a 'picturesque' poet 'of sensation rather than reflection', he was drawing on the tradition of picturesque speculation which had its beginnings in the 1780s with William Gilpin and others. The picturesque began as a mode of describing painting and natural landscapes, but by Hallam's time it was an accepted term for the judgment of poetry as well. But by 1831, at least for Hallam's purposes, the meaning has significantly changed. Hallam contrasts Shelley and Keats with Wordsworth – who has written, Hallam says, much that is 'good as philosophy, powerful as rhetoric, but false as poetry'. Wordsworth is a poet who will 'pile his thoughts in a rhetorical battery . . . instead of letting them flow in a natural course of contemplation'; he will 'seek for images to illustrate [his] conceptions'. But Keats and Shelley 'had no need to seek; they lived in a world of images; for the most important and extensive portion of their life consisted in those emotions which are immediately conversant with sensation. . . . Hence they are not descriptive, they are

picturesque.' By setting Keats, Shelley, and Tennyson above Wordsworth in tendency rather than in achievement, Hallam demands a
poetry that will be all 'spots of time', a total or pure substance without rhetoric or unabsorbed moralizing. Hallam quite under-
standably wants whole poems, a unification of sensibility of the sort
that would preclude the narrative tags which end the fragments
'There was a Boy' and 'Nutting', and where the confusions of Book
VIII of *The Prelude* would be less naked.

Hallam's critique obliges us to defend Wordsworth as a poet who
did often resort willy-nilly to logical enunciation if he felt it was
appropriate – a poet who felt the price was worth paying. 'Tintern
Abbey' itself constitutes a defence that descriptive and reflective
modes of the mind may work in unison, and that conceptual thought
is equally as important as behaviour in a poetry which is, to borrow
Coleridge's phrase, more than usual emotion and more than usual
order. 'To Toussaint L'Ouverture' (1802) is among the finest of
Wordsworth's landscape pieces because by a *tour de force* it applies the
larger Wordsworthian landscape to politics:

> Toussaint, the most unhappy man of men!
> Whether the whistling Rustic tend his plough
> Within thy hearing, or thy head be now
> Pillowed in some deep dungeon's earless den; –
> O miserable Chieftain! where and when
> Wilt thou find patience! Yet die not; do thou
> Wear rather in thy bonds a cheerful brow:
> Though fallen thyself, never to rise again,
> Live, and take comfort. Thou hast left behind
> Powers that will work for thee; air, earth, and skies;
> There's not a breathing of the common wind
> That will forget thee; thou hast great allies;
> Thy friends are exultations, agonies,
> And love, and man's unconquerable mind.

It is all logical enunciation, without a line of pregnant description.
The very insubstantiality of the images from nature gives force to a
contention that the earth itself is antagonized by human wrong and
tyranny. It is like the greater landscape of the Simplon Pass in assert-
ing the vital identity of inner and outer nature.

It is the assertion and enactment of that vital identity which
accounts for the power of Wordsworth's example for writers who
follow. 'Love of Nature leading to Love of Man' may be understood

more generally as the motto of Wordsworth's century. It is no uncommon or random occurrence that John Ruskin, gradually perceiving the mountain gloom while growing at the same time disillusioned about Victorian society, shifts his concern from landscape to architecture, from aesthetics to ethics. When Ruskin says that 'a complete analysis, or anything like it, would involve a treatise on the whole history of the world', he might be speaking of Economics or Comparative Religions – and in a sense he is; but he is here specifically referring to the concept of landscape. *Modern Painters* is perhaps the finest and most comprehensive English critical work in the century, largely because Ruskin is not content to rest in his original premise of landscape: the defence of J. M. W. Turner against charges that the painter was not 'like nature' is more ambitiously subsumed by an inquiry into the state of society, the environment of creation, in nineteenth-century Europe. And after Ruskin, writers like Thomas Hardy and D. H. Lawrence move from the rural novel to a far wider inquiry as their discontent with the social world requires larger structures of critique. The movement may be described either as a progress away from landscape to larger and more adequate genres or modes, or as a stretching of landscape to cope with moral preoccupations which were conveyed in previous centuries by epic, heroic and historical forms. Sooner or later writers found the landscape feeling inadequate, but not before it had induced a radically romantic, visionary sensibility, a passion for naked nature and all the accompanying metaphysical images of exposure.

So against Hallam we may set John Ruskin's homage: 'Wordsworth's distinctive work was a war with pomp and pretence, and a display of the majesty of simple feelings and humble hearts, together with high reflective truth in his analysis of the courses of politics and ways of men; without these, his love of nature would have been comparatively worthless.' Of course, both Hallam and Ruskin are right. Wordsworth risked his poetry itself to make its function unmistakably moral. The poetry could not have been written if these larger predilections were expunged. Often in Wordsworth the struggle against the implied purity of the landscape genre means earning moral maturity, but it also makes for lapses on behalf of desperate sincerity, for ambiguity and grotesquerie as well as greatness. The morality of meditative observation, profoundly anti-social at times, and ideally wider than mere society because of 'the gravitation and the filial bond' that connect man 'with the world', makes for poetic effects very much in the unfashionable

manner of enunciation and overt statement. But Wordsworth is in
this respect most fortunately incorrigible. As the greatest of landscape poets he is also the most impure.

Select bibliography

BEACH, J. W., The Concept of Nature in Nineteenth-Century English Poetry, New York, 1936; reprinted 1966.

CLARK, K., Landscape Into Art, London, 1949, reprinted 1952, Boston, 1961.

CLARKE, C. C., Romantic Paradox, London, 1962; New York, 1963.

COHEN, R., The Art of Discrimination: Thomson's 'The Seasons' and the Language of Criticism, London, 1964; Berkeley (Calif.), 1963.

COLERIDGE, S. T., Biographia Literaria, ed. J. Shawcross, Oxford, 1907.
——Collected Letters, 2 vols., ed. Earl Leslie Griggs, Oxford, 1956.
——Notebooks, ed. K. Coburn, New York, 1957; London, 1962.

DAVIE, D., Purity of Diction in English Verse, London, 1952; rev. edn. 1967; New York, 1967.
——Articulate Energy, London, 1955.

DE VERE, A., 'Remarks on the Personal Character of Wordsworth's Poetry', Transactions of the Wordsworth Society, No. 5, London, 1883.

FERRY, D., The Limits of Mortality, Middletown, Conn., 1959.

FRIEDLÄNDER, M. J., Landscape, Portrait, Still-life, trans. R. F. C. Hull, Oxford, 1949; New York, 1963.

GILPIN, W., Observations on the River Wye and several Parts of South Wales, etc., relative Chiefly to Picturesque Beauty, London, 1782.

HALLAM, A., Review of Tennyson's Poems of 1830 in The Englishman's Magazine, 1831; reprinted in Tennyson: The Critical Heritage, ed. J. D. Jump, London 1967.

HARTMAN, G. H., The Unmediated Vision, New Haven, 1954.
——Wordsworth's Poetry 1787–1814, New Haven and London, 1964.

93

Select bibliography

HAYDON, B. R., *The Diary of B. R. Haydon,* 5 vols., ed. W. B. Pope, Cambridge, Mass., 1960.

HULME, T. E., *Speculations,* 2nd edn., ed. H. Read, London, 1936; reprinted 1958; New York, 1963.

JONES, J., *The Egotistical Sublime: A History of Wordsworth's Imagination,* London, 1954; New York, 1964.

NICHOLSON, N., *The Lakers: The Adventures of the First Tourists,* London, 1955.

NOYES, R., *Wordsworth and the Art of Landscape,* Bloomington, Ind., 1968.

PALGRAVE, F. T., *Landscape in Poetry from Homer to Tennyson,* London 1897.

PERKINS, D., *The Quest For Permanence,* Cambridge, Mass., 1959.
———*Wordsworth and the Poetry of Sincerity,* Cambridge, Mass., 1964.

RUSKIN, J., *Modern Painters,* comprising vols. 1–5 of *Works,* 39 vols., ed. E. T. Cook and A. Wedderburn, Library Edition, London, 1903–1912.

WASSERMAN, E., *The Subtler Language,* Baltimore, 1959.

WESLING, D., 'Ruskin and the Adequacy of Landscape', *Texas Studies in Literature and Language,* vol. IX, no. 2, Summer 1967.
———'The Inevitable Ear: Freedom and Necessity in Lyric Form, Wordworth and After', *English Literary History,* vol. 36, No. 3 (The Johns Hopkins Press, Baltimore, September 1969).

WILBUR, R., 'Poetry and the Landscape', *The New Landscape,* ed. G. Keypes, Chicago, 1956.

WORDSWORTH, CHRISTOPHER, D. D., *Memoirs of the Life of William Wordsworth,* 2 vols., London, 1851.

WORDSWORTH, WILLIAM, *Guide to the Lakes,* 1835 version, ed. E. de Selincourt, Oxford, 1906.

Index

Index

Hartman, Geoffrey, 62
Haydon, Benjamin Robert, frontis-
piece and 84–5
Hopkins, G. M., 1
Hulme, T. E., 1, 5, 6, 7, 18

'I wandered lonely as a cloud', 10,
76
'Idiot Boy, The', 9

James, William, 73
Jarrell, Randall, 6
Jefferies, Richard, 64
Johnson, Samuel, 3–4, 25
Jones, John, 61, 87

Kant, Immanuel, 59
Keats, John, 28, 52, 59, 89–90

Lacey, Norman, 80
Lawrence, D. H., 88, 91
'Letter to Mathetes', 85
'Lines left upon a Seat', 74–9
Lyrical Ballads, 8, 9–10, 15, 41, 61

'Michael', 73, 87–8
Mill, J. S., 7
Milton, John, 27, 84, 88–9

Nicholson, N., 40–1
'Night Piece, A', 9
'Nutting', 36, 68–9, 90

'Ode: Intimations of Immortality',
73
'Old Cumberland Beggar, The',
44–6, 47

Palgrave, Francis Turner, 7
Peter Bell, 81

Poems on the Naming of Places, 64–5
67–9
Pope, Alexander, 5
Pound, Ezra, 1, 5
Prelude, The, 1, 2, 3, 6, 9, 12, 16, 17,
21, 30–1, 33, 35–44, 46–7, 52–7,
61, 62, 66–7, 69–71, 72, 77, 79,
80–9, 90
Price, Uvedale, 13

Recluse, The, 10, 30, 61, 62–4
'Resolution and Independence', 32,
48–50
Rousseau, J. J., 59
Ruskin, John, 17, 91

Scott, Walter, 32
Shairp, J. C., 7
Shakespeare, William, 2, 20, 78
Shelley, P. B., 89–90
Stephen, Leslie, 7
Stevens, Wallace, 8

Tennyson, Alfred Lord, 89–90
Thomson, James, 3, 5–6, 15, 18, 25
'Tintern Abbey', 1, 5, 9, 19, 22–9,
30, 51, 52, 70, 72, 74, 77, 78,
79, 90
'To Toussaint L'Ouverture', 90
Turner, J. M. W., 31, 91

Wasserman, Earl, 5
'White Doe of Rylstone, The', 66,
67, 72
Wilbur, Richard, 65
Wilson, Richard, 59, 60
'With ships the sea was sprinkled
far and nigh', 9
'Written in March', 49

Young, Edward, 27